...YOU SHOULDN'T HAVE JOINED

BOB CLARKE CCB

Cover art and caricature: Chris Price

Illustrations: Sean Mark Stone

Design and typeset: Amy Alldred
www.amyalldred.co.uk

Printed by Srinivas Fine Arts (P) Ltd, Sivakasi, India
www.srinivasfinearts.com

Order form can be obtained online from www.ifyoucanttakeajoke.co.uk

1126

One good mother is worth
100 school masters and
10,000 facebook friends

Acknowledgements

Roger Alldred who encouraged me to write down a few of my yarns which have snowballed into this book.

Chris Price for creating front cover and caricature.

Shaun Mark Stone, Illustrator. Usually paints landscapes using oil paint and doesn't know his oars from his rowlocks regarding things naval. Just the man, I thought, to depict nautical scenes using watercolours. His submarines are in a class of their own!

Kassy (Clarke) Alldred for processing my scribble, and for tolerating continual alterations and additions. For dotting the I's, crossing the T's and keeping me to the point. Surely that's what sisters are for, isn't it?

Amy Alldred, Graphic Designer. With the precision of a master gunner and the vision of a masthead lookout!

'Ram' Ramachandran of Srinivas Fine Arts (P) Ltd, for production advice.

Thanks for supporting my book & for helping service charities.

Best regards

Bob Gale

My thanks for the enthusiastic support of the many secretaries and members of the Royal Naval Association, Submarine Association and of numerous Royal British Legion clubs throughout the UK.

A special thanks to Mr Philip (Darby) Allen MBE of the HMS St Vincent Association. Ex-boy seamen and other naval trainees are kindred spirits having endured the struggle to ascend from the bottom rung.

To those mentioned by name in my book I honour and cherish the memory of their actions.

Ingredients of a Matelots yarn
A Mix of memories
The bare bones of facts
A touch of spice
A few drops of rum
And more than a pinch of salt.

PART 1

A Year At HMS St Vincent
Boys' Training Establishment

I pay you to post them through The doors not to read them

As quoted from Mr Harvey, Harvey's Newsagents

January 1950, the submarine HMS Truculent was accidently rammed and sunk by the Dutch coaster Davina in the Medway estuary. I was about eleven years old when I saw the Truculent at Thomas Wards yard at Grays beach. She had been salvaged from where she was sunk and brought to Grays to be scrapped. The sight of her lying there had spurred my interest to find out the facts of the tragic accident. What saddened me most was that all of those formerly trapped inside on the seabed had managed to escape only to perish in the harsh, cold conditions on the surface. If they had ensured that rescue craft were on station above ready to take them aboard most, if not all of them, would have survived.

It wasn't long after having seen the Truculent that I was delivering papers through the letterboxes around Chadwell-St-Mary when I noticed the headlines that the six year old submarine HMS Affray had failed to surface south of the Isle of Wight. The next day she was feared lost with all hands. I read the reports every day as a massive sonar search was carried out to locate her. She had seventy five persons on board, her crew had been reduced to fifty to help accommodate twenty one officer trainees and four royal marines. The search continued for several weeks and she was eventually found in an area called the Hurd

1

deep. She was lying intact on the bottom with the exception of the snort mast which although broken was hanging by a slither. It seemed that the boat was quickly flooded by a massive inrush of water through the broken snort tube affording no time to shut off a compartment to allow escape attempts. All hatches were firmly shut, the indicator buoys were still in their wells. If they had been released searching vessels would have been able to locate her quickly. No attempt was made to salvage the Affray, she has a protected status as the grave for all on board and cannot be disturbed.

These tragic accidents interested me as even at this early age thoughts of 'going to sea' had been downloaded to my hard drive. The prospect of a career with Thomas Bata Shoes or Ford Motors or at any one of the local factories or utilities where most of my school chums ended up filled me with dread.

I wanted to be in the Navy, as a gunner perhaps, but to be in submarines seemed to me then to be akin to signing one's own death warrant.

It was usual to leave school during that era at the end of the term following one's fifteenth birthday, so I left when the school broke up for Christmas 1954. I had already been to the recruiting office in Grays to enquire about joining the Navy and then after passing initial tests to the main recruiting centre near Trafalgar Square in London for other tests, a medical and eyesight checks.

I knew that the Navy wouldn't allow me in until the age of fifteen and three months which was their policy, so I got a job at the Co-op grocery shop along the parade at Blackshots, less than a two mile walk from home. I used to help the driver with home delivery of groceries in their Austin A70 van, a novelty in those days to be driven around because the average family did not own a car.

I also remember quartering up the huge cheese rounds with a wire cutter and doing other odd jobs around the shop. My pay enabled me to buy some decent clothes to join up in, as I knew we would have to wear our own clothes for a while until we received our uniform issue and I didn't want to be looked down on by anybody. I think I was a bit sensitive in those days.

Thank you ma'am, sorry Sam

A stiff westerly breeze on this bleak February morning whipped up the spray – I could taste the salt – as the powerful diesel of the harbour launch accelerated it away from the ferry pontoon by Portsmouth harbour station.

I looked across the row of young, slightly apprehensive looking recruits seated along the bench seats on either side of the launch. I wondered if they were as nervous and excited as myself – some looked hard and tough, others as if they already regretted having signed up. Some I had met earlier at the Navy Recruiting Centre near Trafalgar Square, they had travelled down with me on the train. Others who joined us at Portsmouth were from other southern counties of England and the Channel Islands. Those from the north, the west and from Scotland and Ireland we would meet later at HMS St Vincent, the boys' training establishment at Gosport.

This was already an adventure for me having taken the longest rail journey of my fifteen years of life. The water here looked clear and green as opposed to the black oily looking Thames at Tilbury where I had trained as a Sea Cadet.

My father, Bill Clarke, was sent to sea in the Merchant Marine at the age of fifteen and served through both world wars and the years between. He had been torpedoed and sunk by a German submarine in each of those wars. In September 1942 he was adrift in a lifeboat for twelve days and nights and lucky to survive. My two elder brothers, Ken (aged 18 years) and John (16 years), like many other boys locally, had joined the Merchant Marine shortly after leaving school and were already away at sea. I tracked their ships movements by reading the Lloyds Shipping Reports at Grays library.

The annual 'Navy Days' at Chatham dockyard had fired my enthusiasm for the Royal Navy.

With her pristine pale grey paintwork, dark green anti-slip pads on her metal decks and the scrubbed wood planking on her quarterdeck, the cruiser – Superb – caught my eye. Unbeknown to mc she was destined to be my first ship. I would be carrying on the hard work of keeping her in that condition. The Superb along with the lean mean looking destroyers, bristled with weapons. With their smart, weather-beaten, cheerful and confident crews, these were the greyhounds of the ocean. This quiet, shy lad was determined to be their equal.

I watched the efficient crew of the launch as we crossed the harbour, they were all retired wartime Navy men. To our starboard an aircraft carrier, moored to the jetty, had her aircraft ranged on deck. Ahead of us a frigate under tow, with her armament cocooned in plastic, was being taken into reserve. On our port side at HMS Dolphin I could see sinister looking submarines, four abreast at the jetties. Little did I know then that most of my service life would be spent aboard these craft.

Our launch entered the Clarence victualing yard where R.F.A. (Royal Fleet Auxiliary) tankers and supply ships were based. Disembarking we boarded an R.N. bus waiting to take us to St Vincent and it wasn't long before we were entering the arched gateway to what would be our uncomfortable home for the next year. The bus stopped outside a three storey building which we found out was the 'nozzers' (new entries) block. In six weeks this 'home from home' should turn us schoolboy landlubbers into erstwhile naval ratings – they would break our backs trying anyway. We sat on wooden benches along wooden tables. Everything looked scrubbed and spotless – it wouldn't be long before we found out who kept things this way.

As tea was served I realized how tired and hungry I was after the day's travel and excitement. Thick sliced bread, curious 'rounds' of margarine and a tin of fish paste – my favourite (my dad's nickname for me was 'pasty face'. He called all of us kids after racing greyhounds).

A petty officer introduced himself as our instructor. He was a blue eyed west countryman, his row of medals testimony of his war service. I thought he was going to give us some stirring Nelson-like welcoming speech, instead this is what he said:-

"There were two buck rabbits, the grizzled old Sam and the sprightly young Jack. A line of comely young does waited to be serviced. Young Jack rabbit said "Sam, you start at the far end and I'll start at this end", Jack was quick off the mark, eager to get his fair share. "Thank you ma'am, thank you ma'am, sorry Sam, thank you ma'am, thank you ma'am".

It wasn't much longer before, having stowed our gear in our metal locker which was alongside our assigned bed, the bugler was playing 'last post' as we turned in. Sleep would be precious and we would get little enough of it. Our life in future would be dictated by bugle call over the tannoy system. Still at least I didn't have to share a bed with two of my brothers again although I would be sharing a dorm with 25 other youngsters, none of whom I yet knew, but had the feeling that we would become a band of brothers – us against 'them'. 'Them' being instructors, officers, ship's company and even the civilian employees of the training base. We were on the same level as the ship's cat. Everything we did would be under scrutiny. To survive we had to help each other, which on reflection is the basis of any effective team or organisation.

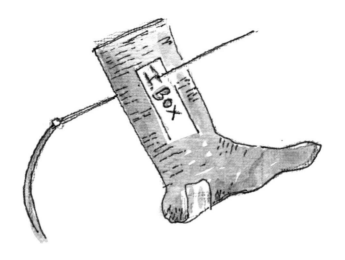

A housewifes Work is never done

The next weeks were hectic and confusing. Nobody referred to the Navy, we were in the Andrew. Andrew Miller, a zealous press gang officer during the Napoleonic wars, impressed so many men into the King's Navy that he was said to own the Royal Navy. The Andrew was now our mum and dad. The Andrew would dress us, feed us, pay us and if they thought it best for us, could stop our pay. They had a range of other punishments to help our development. Poor parade ground drill could result in an individual, or the whole squad, doubling around the parade ground until the GI (gunnery instructor who was a god-like figure to us – the God of Wrath – he was completely unbending, thinking only of the good of the Andrew and of the ships he would one day have to release us to). Where was I, oh yes, still doubling round the parade ground. Eventually the GI would think it had done us enough good and we would resume our drill. Poor rifle drill would result in the same doubling around but this time with a rifle held over the head, arms outstretched. It had a side benefit, not appreciated at the time, of helping our physical development. Everything the GI did, he told us, was for our benefit.

I will say this now. I never experienced or saw any bullying while in the service and our instructors showed no favour – they hated us all – they used the carrot and stick method without the carrots!

I can't remember in which order, but we had eye tests, they were big on colour blindness, audio tests, medical tests and the first of numerous injections. I was surprised as we had most of these tests to get in the Navy but as a boy seaman second class one doesn't argue. The ship's cat was superior to us.

Next we drew kit. We weren't actually measured for uniforms, only by the storekeeper's experienced eyes as we filed past him. Without boring you to tears, uniforms were numbered from No. 1's down to something like No. 10's, some being variations of the other. We had uniforms and accessories for arctic regions and across the spectrum to tropical dress. In those days we wore white summer hats and in the winter black and we had a large round metal hat box to keep them in. We had a Burberry raincoat and a heavy greatcoat, shoes, boots, light evening shoes, plimsolls, seamanship manual, knife, gas mask, hammock and a huge kitbag as well as a sturdy leather-edged suitcase.

We learnt that most things supplied to us from the stores were known as 'pussers issue'. Our seaman's clasp knife became our 'pussers dirk', our shoes were 'pussers crabs', the long bars of browny yellow clothes washing soap was known by all as 'pussers hard', but the washing of clothing was termed 'dhobeying' – taken from the Indian name for a washer-man. The word pusser is a derivation of purser. Although there hasn't been such a rank in the Andrew since before Jellicoe was a boy, the supply officer of a warship or base is nicknamed 'the purser'.

Most trades or professions use slang terms, but in the Navy there are so many that it becomes almost another language the use of which would render the book almost impossible to understand for the layman.

Even then as a naïve youngster I knew we wouldn't use much of this kit during our year's training, or on our first ship, we would only need the kit for whichever weather extreme it would operate in. Much of what we drew I also realised, that before we came to use it, we would have outgrown it.

What I didn't know in my naivety was that kit wasn't necessarily for wearing or using – it was for sewing names in, for dhobeying, for pressing for mustering and most importantly for having inspected. One important item I have missed is 'the housewife'. This item of kit was a cloth roll which contained scissors, cotton, needles, buttons and a roll of white tape. We each made up a name stamp by fixing together the initials of our Christian names plus our surname, each rubber letter was mounted on individual wooden blocks that were then glued together. All kit was then stamped with our names or onto a piece of white tape the length of the name– easy. The hard part followed. Each clothing item first had to have the name stamped tape sewn on to it. Every shirt, white front, pair of trousers, coat, jacket, each sock (we had socks for all occasions – black, white tropical, sports – a few pairs of each), dozens of items in total. Having stamped our name on the tape, sewn the tape onto each item of uniform we then had to stitch around each letter in chain stitch using blue thread.

It was then it dawned on us that names mattered. Boy Seaman I (Wooden) Box had a distinct advantage over boy seaman R.M. (Paddlearse) Rowbotham. Mine, R.T. (Bobbie) Clarke was kind of middling.

Our new 'dad' GI (Razor) Sharpe named us on behalf of the Andrew. To many he gave the standard service nicknames – Edwards were 'Bungy', Collins 'Jumper', White 'Knocker' or 'Chalky'. When he came to Clark or Clarke there were three of us. That didn't stump 'Razor'. J. Clark he named as 'Nobby', R (Robin) Clark he christened 'Robbie', me R. T. Clarke he decreed to be 'Bobbie'. Thus we all had new names most of which followed us throughout our service. It was a kind of homogenising process divorcing us from our previous lives. It didn't matter any more if you were a 'council house kid' like myself, or from a middle class background. Your previous 'status' counted for nothing. We now dressed the same, the individual's own efforts could make him look smarter. We fed the same, for some it was better food than they were used to. We used toilet paper, not the torn up newspaper some used at home and for the first time I had my own tube of toothpaste rather than using soap and salt – things weren't all bad. The toothpaste tube and the box it came in were both plain white. Each had R.N. printed boldly in dark blue on both sides. I think it was to remind us each morning that we were in the Navy and not swanning around on daddy's yacht, an easy mistake to make! We were from all parts of the UK and Eire, plus a few from the Commonwealth. It didn't matter from where, we were now a class of equals.

If in danger, if in doubt

We spent a lot of time in the gym doing all sorts of physical training – free-standing and on wall bars. We played medicine ball, vaulted horses and climbed ropes – an essential skill to master for a seaman.

Navy physical training instructors are known as 'club swingers', or 'clubs' for short, on account of the crossed clubs insignia they wore on their 'T' shirts and other uniforms. They believed that boxing was good for our soul. To this end they would pair us off, each pair was then expected to get in the ring and pummel the hell out of each other for a couple of minutes. The only actual coaching I remember being given was when clubs said "If in danger, if in doubt, always stick your left hand out". With that clubs jabbed out his left fist and floored the lad standing right in front of him. My policy of burying myself in the midst of the pack stood me in good stead once again.

I remember my first bout. My opponent, Stewart, was a lad about six inches taller than me. He came out at the bell, his arms swinging like a windmill and I took a few punches. I knew that unless I could get inside his reach I was going to be decimated. I ducked down low and managed to get in close. I was able to land a few blows which looked hard enough to satisfy clubs but had no intention of hurting Stew, as a couple of days before he had bulled the toecaps of my boots for me.

These boots, as issued, had a rough plammishcd surface, unlike the smooth easy to polish leather of officers shoes or those of a normal, semi-sane person. The toe caps had to be 'spit and polished' to build up a mirror-like finish which is what we called bulling. Our P.O. wanted to see his face in them. God knows why, he had the face of a gargoyle which even a mother would struggle to love. I've always liked clean shoes but the bulling was a step too far.

I paid Stew back in a number of ways. I wasn't any smarter than him but I was quicker and speed was often of the essence, not only with the instructors, but with a class of boys trying to elbow their way to the prime positions. These positions for me would be a spot where it was difficult for the instructor to single me out, or a place nearest the door if for instance we needed to rush out at the end of the session and get near the front of a mealtime queue. I would hold on to a seat next to me, by fair means or foul, until Stew ambled along with no sense of urgency. Eight years after leaving St Vincent, Stew and I met up at the Seamanship School in Portsmouth. We were both on the same qualifying course for Petty Officer. He was a Leading Surveyor in the Hydrographers Department, which suited his slow methodical temperament. He could leave me standing in chart work and navigation which I had regarded as my forte.

Maybe Stew was slow and methodical at work because he reserved his energies for more pressing matters – in six years of marriage he'd produced four children!

Water Babies

Strangely enough being able to swim was not a requirement for joining the Navy. I can't remember it even being mentioned. Perhaps the recruiters knew something we didn't.

Swimming has been a favourite exercise and pastime for most of my life. The earliest swims I can remember were at the old Exmouth Baths, an old ramshackle corrugated iron covered building, built over and jutting out into the Thames at Grays beach. It got its name from the 'Exmouth' training ship anchored in the Thames close by.

Later on my two elder brothers and I used to cross on the Tilbury ferry to Gravesend where there was a really good outdoor pool. Our father, who was a strong swimmer, would often swim there as well. The pool and my father now only live on in memories.

The ferry left Tilbury's landing stage - the entry point for many immigrants en route to London; the exit for emigrants bound for Australia aboard the Orient and P & O liners. The ornate Gravesend town pier where we landed is the world's oldest surviving cast iron pier, built in 1834. It was only a short walk from there to the pool, the area around which had been rebuilt by General Gordon, the famous Scottish soldier who commanded the engineers, while also rebuilding the New Tavern Fort. General Gordon as Governor of the Sudan was killed at Khartoum in 1885 trying to quell the uprising by the Mahdi.

Floating came naturally to me. As a toddler my brothers had taken me to a local sand quarry half full of water. So intent were they on sailing their imagined ships - bits of wood – that it came as quite a surprise to see me floating on my back toward the centre of the quarry. Their shouts of alarm attracted the attention of a passer by an off-duty policeman who pulled me out of the water.

St Vincent had a good pool, I think it is still there to this day, even though most of the other buildings are long gone.

Club swingers were good all-rounders, good boxing coaches and no nonsense swimming instructors. "Line up round the deep end lads. When I blow my whistle jump in and tread water", ordered clubs. "But I can't swim sir", called out one of the non-swimmers. "Don't worry you soon will son", reassured clubs. As usual he was right. Within a few weeks all of us could do a couple of lengths wearing overalls and plimsolls. To my knowledge no boys were ever lost to drowning.

Breakfast at Tiffany's
lumps and all

We always had porridge. Well if we didn't it seemed like we did. Not the thick, creamy porridge that we boiled in a saucepan at home, creamy because we stirred a couple of spoons of condensed milk into it. Navy porridge was a thin gruel of oats and water plus a few lumps and a pinch of salt, but we grew to like it, or at least we ate it. A case of like it or lump it.

Some days it was followed by sausage and tinned tomatoes or bacon and beans or perhaps a boiled egg, occasionally we would have 'spit-head pheasant' the matelot's term for a kipper. My favourite was what the boys called 'shit on a raft'. This was chopped kidneys in thick gravy on fried bread. We always ate as if it was our last meal. We were always hungry, burning calories faster than we could replace them as we did everything on the double.

After breakfast we'd check our bed space, making sure our blankets were folded in the regulation manner and placed at the head of the bed under the pillow, on top of the blue and white bedcover which had to be pulled taut with its anchor emblem dead centre. Then a quick check of our locker which we never locked. Its contents had to be folded seaman-ship manual size and stowed in a set manner. The socks would be inside out, folded so the blue thread embroidered, name-stamped white tape, which we'd stitched to the inside of each sock, was on show for when the Duty P.O. came round to check the dorm while we were away being indoctrinated with other essential mundungus. To return after dinner and find the bedding strewn on the floor was an indication that the P.O. was not best pleased with your efforts.

After checking and folding our kit we would check our appearance in the full length mirrors to see that the clothing we had pressed the previous evening was sitting on our body as it should, fully buttoned, cap tally square with the 'T' of 'ST' in 'HMS ST VINCENT' in line with the nose, long gaiters tightly laced, boots polished. We could then go down and make ready for the morning skirmish and look forward to what the day had in store for us.

Six years later alongside at Dolphin, the submarine base, we used to go inboard to the Dining Hall which we nicknamed 'Tiffany's' after seeing the film 'Breakfast At Tiffany's' whose main character was Holly Golightly. I served with two overweight brothers who were unkindly nicknamed the Golightly's. I never met the film stars but I did see the film. The Golightly's weren't film stars they were stokers, heavyweights in their field. The porridge was still made to the same recipe.

Skirmishing the parade ground

The parade ground was hallowed ground. We were allowed to drill on it and parade on it. That was all. We had to double round its perimeter, no matter how urgent the errand we couldn't cross it. Only officers and instructors could walk across the parade ground.

Each morning, before the morning parade, we had to skirmish the area. To do this we formed a line abreast, spaced out at arms width and crossed the area with eyes down to see and remove every item of litter. Bear in mind that this had been done every day since Jellicoe was a boy, well almost. Smoking near the parade ground and the dropping of litter were capital offences, so, apart from the odd leaf or bird dropping, there wasn't much to find.

Recently Roger, my brother-in-law, a man blessed with much common sense, asked me if 'they' were serious or just having a joke with us. Try as I might I couldn't convince him that this was a matter of national naval importance.

A birds eye view

Morning parade involved an inspection of whatever rig we were wearing that day. Each class would be dressed appropriately for their particular activities, then after the parade classes would double off to carry them out.

One day our class embussed to the naval air station at nearby Lee-on-Solent, for most of us this would be our first flight. The aircraft, a De Havilland Dominie, was the naval version of the Dragon Rapide, which was designed in the 1930's. It had a double wing and a roomy cabin which seated about eight of us. We trundled off the grass track and were almost immediately over the Solent and Isle of Wight. We turned left, crossed over the outer spit and followed the coast along the Southsea front and Portsmouth dockyard, turning left again to pass over Gosport. We could see St Vincent under our right wing and were soon touching down again at Lee. Everything seemed so close together from the air, you had a bird's eye view and flew as the crow flies, or should I say, as the Dragon Rapide does. This was reinforced a year later when dealing with military aircraft which flew many times the speed of our double winged Dominie. I tried to visualise the jet pilot's bird's eye view, as my spoken instructions directed him to achieve an airborne intercept or toward a ground target, as he closed our radars contacts at speed.

This short flight had given us boys a perspective that few, if any, had experienced before, which was probably its reason.

I noticed many things during the flight, the first was the rifle range at Browndown[1] which I could see to port (left) as we took off. The ranges were on marginal land, a type of stony scrub between Stokes Bay and the airfield at the Alverstoke end of Gosport. Being next to the Solent was an ideal spot for a rifle range – an exclusion zone for security and safety from wayward ordnance could easily be set up here. The canny cod probably preferred this set up to the fisherman though.

We often went to these ranges to practice firing the weapon we'd drilled with the previous weeks. You may have thought that the Lee-Enfield[2] rifle was merely a weapon of warfare, but we knew it to be a tool

---

[1]Browndown had been used by the military for over 500 years. It was used during WWI to practice trench warfare and during WWII as a Royal Marines base. It was a marshalling area for 'D' day.

21

the G.I. used to strip away our individuality. It was a tool he used with menacing effectiveness to gel us into a squad, ensuring that rifle butts resounded in unison as brass met asphalt on the parade ground. The remedy, for those that failed to gel during drill, was a doubling round the parade ground perimeter, with arms stretched out above the head, holding your rifle. As your arms buckled and trembled under the rifle's weight you prayed that the G.I. would consider his thoughtful remedy had worked its magic and you could take your place back amongst the squad.

When it came to rifles I think most of us boys were cowboys at heart and like me had shot from the saddle of our make-believe horses with our wooden stick Winchester 73's, point and fire, point and fire, red Indians toppling like nine-pins. The Navy's method was slightly different. First we learned the working parts and how to strip and reassemble them. How to oil and clean the gun using the pull-through and oiler stored in a recess of the brass plate at the end of the butt, the very same brass plate that we had to strike on the ground in split second unison as did the rest of the squad. We learnt how to set and adjust the sights, to load and reload the magazine in quick time and how to care for the ammunition.

Our attention was then directed to the range itself, to the butts and

---

[2]The Lee-Enfield rifle which fires a .303 round is the world's longest serving infantry rifle, used by the British military and by many Commonwealth countries from 1895 to 1957. It is still used by some, notably the Indian police and the Canadian Rangers Arctic Reserves. The bolt system was designed by Lee and the gun manufactured at the Royal Small Arms factory at Enfield. Over 17 million were produced.

to the targets. How, when it came to our turn to work in the butts, we would raise and lower these targets and how we would indicate the position the round had impacted or if it had missed. This indication was the pointer that the firer used to adjust his sights.

All the while all we wanted to do was fire the blooming thing and prove what 'dead eyed dicks' we were. But no, not yet, we had to lie in the prone firing position – get the stance correct, make a comfortable but firm anchorage with the legs and also with the elbows, keeping the butt tight to the shoulder, cheek close in, eye lining up the back and foresight centre of target, keeping the barrel steady – or trying to - before taking first pressure on the trigger.

The G.I. walked down the line of prone riflemen, his boot prodding the legs apart of those not in what he deemed a secure anchorage. By now barrels were beginning to waiver. "You're like a maid with her first dick in her hand" he bawled at one boy. That set all our barrels waivering, as we choked back our laughter, for fear of becoming a target ourselves. We just wanted to fire the ruddy things.

Eventually we got to fire from 800yds then later 1,000, if my failing memory serves me correctly. I found that I could often get the first couple of rounds pretty close to the bullseye, but diminishing concentration meant that it was pretty difficult to put 10 rounds down without splattering the outer edges of the target. I would not gain a marksman badge, which worried me not. In a life or death situation, I reasoned, if I could drop or injure my foe with the first couple I'd be happy – I wouldn't want to shoot him to bits.

We gained altitude, on this my first flight, to what I guessed to be about 500ft from my flying experience, sum total about five minutes and we turned over the Isle of Wight crossing over Ryde then turning again somewhere near Bembridge to pass over spitsands fort. The boy sitting to my right was talking into my ear something about 'how like cotton wool the clouds were'. I was next to him in body, but my mind was elsewhere. I had nabbed the seat next to a window and as close to the pilot as I could. I was ready to grab the controls and bring the plane in to land should the pilot suffer some kind of seizure. I knew how to fly. Biggles, courtesy of Captain W. E. Johns, was my heroic flying tutor. I'd understudied Cats-eyes Cunningham, Peter Twiss and Neville Duke and had watched as John Moynihan had landed his Spitfire on our back field. But all that was not in my thoughts. I looked below watching a myriad of sailing dinghies rounding a buoy, like moths around a lamp. I could picture Hawke at Quiberon, Nelson at Aboukir bay and dozens of ships leaving these waters heading for the mulberry harbours at the Normandy beaches.

My flight of fantasy was brought back to earth by the sight of St Vincents mast and the reality that tomorrow I had to make my first ascent into its rigging. With hardly a bump we had touched down – the pilot had landed without any assistance from me.

Little did I realize then that within a few years we would be jetting around the world on foreign holidays and that thirty five years later my future family, my wife and two daughters, would buy me a trip on the supersonic 'Concorde', flying at about 1,400 m.p.h. while drinking champagne and eating oysters. This was beyond my wildest imagination then.

One hand for yourself –
one hand for the ship

I heard about the mast, the Ganges mast that is, while at sea cadets. Our cadets hut and our boats were in the docks at Tilbury, a stronghold of the Merchant Navy. My father had sailed from here on many a voyage in war and in peace. After his last ship was torpedoed and he had survived twelve days in an open lifeboat, he was employed working on PLUTO (pipe line under the ocean) which was being constructed in preparation for the invasion of the continent, to pump fuel oil to keep the allied armies mobile when they landed at Normandy.

This was being done in secret at the Grays end of the docks. Both of my elder brothers left the cadets to go on to the M.N. sea training schools and a few of the other older cadets went to the Royal Navy Training School, H.M.S. Ganges.

From those boys who came back to visit the cadets, I heard of the training and of the mast and how they had to climb it. Now I, like most boys I knew, climbed the tallest trees in our woods. I think most boys are natural climbers, if its there they'll climb it, whereas girls would have to have a reason before doing so. After all we are supposedly linked through evolution to the apes, according to some theories anyway. With this in mind I wasn't particularly fazed by this prospect, or no more so than by the numerous injections I also heard we had to endure.

Once I got to St Vincent and saw the imposing mast, its height dwarfing the accommodation blocks, I knew it would be a challenge. Its presence dominated the parade ground where we drilled, knowing that before long we would be up there amongst the tangle of rigging.

Stories had percolated down to us nozzers about the terrors of the mast. If you fell from the top and were fortunate enough to hit the safety net you would pass through it like a potato through a chipper, but if you missed the net you were ketchup. Thus it wasn't without trepidation we looked forward to our first ascent.

Going to Anson Division from Nozzers you couldn't not think about the mast – it was right outside our dorm window – well its lower portions were. One would have to lean out and crane the neck and look to the heavens to see its top. We didn't see other boys climbing the mast because we would be at our own activities and only in our dorm after the mast climbing was over.

I don't remember my first climb but I think we only got as high as the platform which was about half way up, just above the lower yardarm. This was within my comfort zone, although climbing outwards at an angle to get up onto the platform itself I found nerve wracking at first. The initial climb up to that point was easier than climbing trees, just shinning up the ropework lattice at an easy angle. I think there were boys that had to be encouraged but I don't think they were forced. An actual refusal would take real courage. One thing I soon learnt was that up here us scrawny, wiry little lads could be the equal of the big boys with the booming voices who lorded it on the parade ground. The 'button boy' stood on the truck, the highest point of the mast, with just a rope toggle to hold on to. We all admired him and some aspired to emulate him, but not me. He was a gangling lad you wouldn't pick him out in a crowd.

The next stage was to climb vertically up a wire rope ladder, about 50ft, to reach the upper yardarm, a bit scary as several boys would be clambering up, one after the other. Trouble was if you wanted to stop or to pause those following didn't necessarily want to. Rather than wishing to be thought a bit frightened, which I was, I hauled myself up onto the yardarm and clung to a wire brace close to the mast, trying to look nonchalant. With every subsequent climb I tried to venture a little further out on the yardarm and then to climb up to the top gallant, a smaller yardarm just below the truck. I never felt at ease to sit astride it, swinging my legs and waving to those on the ground like a few of the boys could. I always remember the old adage 'one hand for yourself, one hand for your ship', but sometimes I kept both hands for myself. As regards standing on the button, well I never did or would they could shoot me first but I had the greatest respect for the few boys that did.

Now that the masts are no more I wonder if seamen are any the worse for it, but as I sat on my high perch looking up the creek toward the dockyard and H.M.S. Victory, I thought of the men and boys who had set the sails on this very mast, during the years gone by. I had a sense of pride having mastered this challenge – just got to work out how to get down in one piece!

Dhobey day

Thursday was our dhobeying day. For some reason the best time to do it was at the crack of dawn, or earlier. We were called by the Duty P.O. at 05.00hrs. Possibly it harked back to the time of Nelson or Blake and their lordships of the Admiralty could see no good reason to change it. Tradition dies hard in the Royal Navy.

Who were we to question this? Better to leap out of bed at the first bellow from the P.O. for fear of 'over the mast with bedding' or sluicing out the wash house later. The wash house had a bare concrete floor on which we stood 'bollicky buff' - nude in the layman's terms.

We each used two large galvanized sinks, one with hot water to wash the clothes in, the other with cold to rinse them in. There were none of the modern day detergents to use, instead we used bars of pussers hard soap which had no foaming action. Once each item was washed and rinsed we had to hold it up for the P.O. to inspect. He had been chosen by their lordships to be the sole arbiter of what was clean and what was not. He was warmly clad and wearing seaboots, in his right hand he held a hose, running with cold water, with which to freshen up the holder of a dirty item, before sending him back to remedy it.

We enjoyed breakfast even more on a Thursday!

Smart as guardsmen
– we trained for all eventualities

Our squad was now formed up in 'open order' in other words one extra pace between each of the three ranks. We had just completed a drill manoeuvre known as 'from the halt, to the halt, on the right form squad'. This I believe was last performed by the Grenadier Guards during the Battle of Waterloo but I think the GI, our drill instructor, thought it might be useful to us if we met our French allies at Waterloo or the Gare du Nord. At this stage of our training we knew all of the basic parade ground drills and we would soon be training for St Vincents part during the 'Queen's Birthday Parade' to be held on Southsea Common. Some 300 boy seamen, most in rifle squads of about 30, would take part. We would march behind our bugle band.

The GI's mood seemed unusually jovial as he slowly paced between the ranks to inspect us. "Smart as guardsmen", he said. After a pause he said "Not quite as tall", another pause then he snapped "But twice as intelligent". I nearly dropped my rifle choking back laughter, a few boys laughed openly. The GI's mood immediately changed to one of spitting rage. "During her Majesty's Birthday Parade you will hear all sorts of comments from the crowd, pongos (soldiers) will try to make you laugh, ladies and girls will want to touch your dickeys for luck" (A dickey by the way is not a piece of personal equipment it is the name given to the sailors collar and known by this name probably since Nelson's time).

Doubling around the parade ground with rifles bouncing and our shoulders bruising, helped us to remember his advice. He was a good memory coach, my bruises are long gone, the memory remains.

Earlier that day, before dinner, we had grouped around a ten foot long model of the bow of a warship. That part of the warship known as the forecastle, which in the days of sail and close quarter fighting resembled exactly that, a defensive castle at the fore-end of the ship. Now it was sleek and pointed, designed to cut through the water, giving these ships the speed that would cause them to be known as the greyhounds of the ocean, and giving me the gyp as I lived beneath the bow. The motion of the ship as she buried her nose under heavy seas then rising to meet the next oncoming roller was not unlike a continual rising and falling motion of a busy lift. The model was being used by our seamanship instructor, Chief Petty Officer Barnes, to continue our education of all aspects of anchors, cables and the mooring of ships.

I will never forget his first introduction of himself to us. After telling us his name and rank he said "You will call me Chief, when I say jump you will ask how high Chief?" I listened to him intently as session after session he taught us everything one had to know of the interesting subject. I never once heard him say "Jump" therefore I never found out the height he expected us to jump. What I do know was that after completion of his training I could bring any ship, from the size of an aircraft carrier down to a mickey mouse minesweeper (as we called them) to anchor. As things turned out my main experience would be anchoring or mooring H.M. submarines. The principle was the same although we only carried one 12 cwt anchor and 15 fathoms of chain cable, the associated slips, the capstan and other fittings were standard.

The Chief, as well as his two Petty Officer instructors, would make us conversant with all aspects of seamanship, from taking depth soundings by use of the hand lead line (the means of knowing the depth of water below the ship as we headed up river, or into harbour, toward our moorings) one had to be able to read the marking on the line on the darkest of nights as well as in any weather condition. In conjunction with this we needed to have knowledge of coastal navigation and the shapes and colours of buoys, leading marks and their usage, ships navigation lights and fog signals.

The term 'showing you the ropes' makes me smile inwardly when used by the landlubber who is demonstrating some method of carrying out what is probably a mundane task. Rope and its usage, knots and cordage work, splicing of fibre rope and wire rope, their breaking strains and other properties, is a vast subject, to which we devoted much time and study during the course of our year at St Vincent.

I took a particular interest in a related subject, the use and purchase power of blocks and tackles, the rigging and use of temporary derricks and sheerlegs. This interest stemmed from the times as a boy I used to watch civil defence teams, mainly volunteers, who would practice using this form of rigging to lift heavy parts of collapsed buildings from those who might be trapped below. I have never understood why such a useful organization was disbanded as I am sure their expertise would be a useful aid to civil power following natural disasters or terrorism when regular organisations are stretched to their limits. Still what do we, the hoi polloi, know of these things.

Our instructors pointed out to us that a Royal Navy ship was often the first responder on the scene to give aid or assistance following earthquakes, floods or volcanic eruptions at remote locations worldwide.

Eight years or so to the future I managed to pass this subject during my Petty Officer examinations without having had any further tuition or experience apart from what I learned from them, whereas in other subjects, notably flag signals, sending morse by aldis lamp and semaphore I had to burn much midnight oil to be able to scrape through.

Our further education continued into the evening of two weekdays. Instructor officers schooled us in various subjects which included magnetism and electricity (of which I had little previous knowledge), geography, naval history as well as maths and English. I was by this time an advanced class boy although I can't remember the streaming process for this. It was the result of this extra tuition that I passed a number of the higher education tests (the service equivalent of the GCE 'O' level). Being in a headlong rush to leave school I had no wish to stay on to take exams despite the wishes of my schoolmaster.

All of this is an indication of the need for quite rigid discipline in the lives of young people, especially boys, in regard to education. The boys' training establishments could have a valid place in today's society, not leaning toward seamanship but to the many other skills useful for a man to acquire as well as providing opportunity to take part in adventurous pursuits and sports that many boys do not have the vision, backing or finance needed to try.

The closed establishment provides vital time and space for this process to work, keeping out disruptive influences from without, which would have to include much of the communication technology available to youngsters. Of course this is all pie in the sky the past is gone, unfortunately the good along with the bad.

Attending a St Vincent reunion in recent years I wasn't at all surprised to find out how well in life many of these ex-boy seamen had done not only within the service but in civilian careers afterwards. Very few had fallen by the wayside not being able to cope with hardship, setbacks, the general vicissitudes of life common to us all.

If Cleanliness is next to God liness then We Were Saints

I don't remember getting the Friday feeling, probably because we had little reason to. Firstly because for the first six weeks we were virtual prisoners. Probably that was so the homing instinct could be built, so we would return here, rather than flee back from whence we had come. The only time we saw outside the walls was when marching out of the gate for a mile down to Clarence Yard, where our boats were kept, or when crossing the road outside the gates to the sports fields or medical centre opposite.

Saturday morning after breakfast and parade was for cleaning the accommodation block, the dorm, the stairs and the washroom. It had to be readied for inspection by the Captain, Commander, or someone else close to the almighty.

Now considering we had to keep these areas quite spotless on a daily basis, the Saturday clean was something special, what you might call a deep clean. As you are no doubt aware the strength of a chain is the strength of its weakest link. However much elbow grease you expended on your own task, if the clown cleaning the undersides of the washbasins or down the toilet 'U' bends wasn't up to the mark, we were all 'down the pan', so to speak.

My specialty was the sash window with its small Georgian panes. Being smallish and quite agile I could balance outside on the sill clinging on by my toenails to apply the Bluebell, Brasso, or whatever it was – ours came in a Pusser's issue tin and had no brand name. After application you allowed it to dry to a white powdery finish as it does. By the time I'd done the next window's application, the first one was just ready for buffing off with screwed-up newspaper. God only knows where that came from, as the only newspaper I saw was what my fish and chips were wrapped in, once I was finally allowed ashore for that precious few hours once a week. It's the only place I've ever seen windows cleaned that way – I mean any normal, sane people would do the job quite well with just water. Could be that the Jellicoe family owned the Bluebell mines!

Another major task was bumpering the cortercene – which probably means nothing to you unless you've served time in one of H.M. establishments. Cortercene (I'm not sure of the spelling but I doubt you are either) is a type of lino used by the government 'cos it never wears out. It comes in a brown colour, plain no pattern. The bumper is a heavy block at the end of a long broom-type handle which is affixed to the block by a swivel fitting.

One of our 'chain's' links applies the polish on bended knees. The bumper operator places a pusser's issue cleaning cloth under the block then swings the bumper to and fro with gay abandon until a glass mirror-like finish is achieved. Anyone wishing to traverse the polished surface before the inspection has to either walk on his eyebrows or place cloths under his boots and skate across – either that or risk a severe drubbing.

The rest of our Saturday would be dependent on a successful outcome of the inspection, or it would be back to the drawing board or should I say, the bumper. We were then more or less free, although one always had uniform to maintain. If it was a nice day I would often climb up to the platform of the mast with a book, out of sight should an instructor be looking for a volunteer to perform some extra task that had arisen.

I had been caught out a couple of times when I was detailed to work in the garden of the Captain's house. "Cor you're lucky", said a couple of the boys, "cos the Captain's got a lovely daughter". Mind you neither of them offered to take my place. The house abutted the establishment, built at the same time, same style, same brick. I never saw inside but it was probably more spacious than our dorm which slept almost thirty boys. I never saw the Captain's daughter and I doubt that she saw me. If she did she would only see a weedy gardener or a gardener weeding. After all she was as free as a bird.

I was only ever given a hoe to use for weeding by the grumpy civilian worker who looked after tools and suchlike. To my mind the ground looked as if it needed double digging and levelling, which I had been taught to do at school. I must have gone to one of the few schools that taught boys to do something practical and useful. The garden had probably suffered years of 'weeds' just weeding. Still it gave me a chance to hear some birds sing, around the blocks we only had sparrows, starlings and gulls, not a tuneful note between them.

"Why should Britain tremble"

"Why should Britain tremble"

That was the mocking, scathing comment that our weather-beaten, blue eyed, war decorated, west country Petty Officer Instructor made as he looked along the ranks of us, the raw material he had to turn from nervous, know nothing, just out of school, scrawny recruits into jack tars – hearts of oak, always to be ready, steady boys, steady, ready to fight and to conquer again and again. Well that's the words of the song at least.

It was cold, the March weather had come in like a lamb, warm and gentle all the time we were indoors working to ready our kit, sewing in and marking each item. Now we were out, mustered around the whaler, the seaboat, hoisted and snug at its davits, the cold easterly wind blowing up the creek was laced with some slight icy drizzle. Some of the boys were shivering but not all of us, we thought that if he could stand there explaining the falls, the means by which the boat was raised and lowered into the water and the boat's parts, construction and equipment then we could as well. I had a head start, my father, 'Old Jake' as we brothers called him, he never complained about the weather ever. For all I know the destroyer the P.O. served aboard could have escorted my father's ship as it headed 'Russia bound' in convoy.

If a ship or man was in trouble the seaboat would be called on, whatever the weather condition, to fish the man out of the water, or be used to pass the tow to assist the ship. Funny really the advertising posters showed sailors in exotic locations usually with pretty girls and sun-kissed beaches, perhaps our instructor had got it wrong.

Best we acclimatise to the weather this morning, as after dinner we would be marching down to Clarence Yard to where St Vincents boats were moored. We would be spending one afternoon per week, initially learning to pull (not row as landlubbers called it) the cutters and whalers and then as time progressed to rig and to sail them.

The heavy 32ft cutters had what was known as double banked oars, with two oarsmen per thwart, twelve oarsmen in all each with a fourteen or fifteen foot oar, heavy work for 15 year old striplings. I preferred the 27ft whaler which was propelled by five oarsmen, the boat was narrower and lighter, more manageable and with an in-sync crew, faster. Three oarsmen sat port (left) side with oars out to starboard (right side) the other two sat starboard side with oars out to port. As the oarsmen all faced the stern of the boat they could only see where the boat had been, the only person who could see where the boat was headed was its coxswain.

Eventually we would all get our turn to be the coxswain and explore Fareham creek and much of Portsmouth harbour. This wasn't messing about in boats. We were learning the rule of the road and how to keep out of the way of ferries and warships. We could be under the eye of any of a dozen or so telescopes, from shore or from warships, so any infringement of boating rules or etiquette would be reported to the Duty Officer of HMS St Vincent long before we returned. Woe betide the coxswain if so much as a fender was left dangling over the side of a boat under way.

It would be a few blisters and aches and pains during the learning, but overall I think we all enjoyed it once we mastered the technique.

Modern man who spends money and time in the confines of the gym, pumping iron and walking the treadmill, would benefit more body and soul by being out in the fresh air and open water pulling as a team.

Naval lore says 'a ship is known by its boats'.

Freedom is merely a state of mind

We would be allowed 'ashore' on Saturday the first week then Sunday the following week, not all day mind you, only between the hours of 1300 to 1900. We would have to dress in our No.1 uniform, but that didn't mean you just put it on and strolled out of the gate at any time during those hours.

All shore establishments, known in the Andrew as 'stone frigates', are referred to as HMS – no different to a ship. If you wanted to catch the first 'liberty boat' you would have to muster at the main gate before 1300hrs to be inspected by the duty P.O. This meant that the preceding hour would be spent cleaning shoes to a high shine and pressing the uniform items. I have mentioned the mass of uniform we were issued, much of it quite useless. What I haven't mentioned is the uniform itself and the fact that those who designed it obviously never had to wear or work in it.

Our 'square rig' as it was known bore no resemblance to a civilian suit or the uniform that officers or senior rates wore. Theirs was not unlike a civilian suit with jacket and trousers. Ours retained items that the 'Jack Tar' of Nelson's day would wear such as a blue jean collar with three white stripes around its edge. This would prevent grease from the pigtail staining the uniform jacket or something like that, although with our barbers we didn't have enough hair to have a parting let alone a pigtail. This collar had to be ironed with two outboard and one inboard vertical crease about a hand's width (four inches) apart. Another quite useless item, the silk, was worn under the collar and secured at the front by black tapes, with a bow. A white lanyard, a long piece of cord which in Nelson's day would be used to keep the seaman's knife secure around his waist, had to be worn by us under the collar and looped at the front from under the silk and around this bow. Does this make any sense to you?

To dress first we had to struggle into our white front then pull on the Navy blue serge jumper over our heads the same way naval ratings had done since year splash. In 1957 someone at the Admiralty's fashion department discovered the zip fastener had been invented (although that was back in 1893 word doesn't always travel fast in naval dress design.) We were then issued with jackets with a zip at the front. Until that time Jolly Jack coming offshore alone and inebriated would often sleep in his jacket unable to pull it off over his head without assistance.

As regards the uniform trousers, the bellbottoms as they were known, the pressing of these was an art. First they were turned inside out, then pressed flat to form an inward crease either side, then a fold a hand's width from the bottom and pressed to give a crease across the leg, the same thing was repeated another hand's width above this crease, then re-peated three more times, so in all there were five creases in a concertina form to just below the knee. This I was told was to represent the world's five oceans. It would have been easier to hang a map of them around our necks instead of the lanyard. Once pressed and if not going to be worn straight away we would keep the lower part in its creases and roll up the remainder around it so we could stow it under our mattress. If the bellbottoms were hung up the creases would gradually fall out.

All this pressing would be done without the aid of the modern steam iron, we only had a couple of flat irons to share between the whole dorm, full of boys. Again these trousers never had a zip fly, they had a buttoned flap arrangement for which I never discovered the logic.

An old three badged storeman, a fount of much naval knowledge, had told me that Jellicoe's purser (the pusser in our terms) had bought up the world's supply of rough blue serge material. It must have been down to the last dregs at the time of our issue because in 1957, along with zip fasteners came a finer, easier to press material which could keep a crease for more than a few minutes and was less itchy to wear.

The 'improvements' to uniform included a new issue white cap with plastic top. No longer would we need to use Blanco for whitening not only the cap but also the belts and gaiters we wore when forming a rifle guard when great care had to be taken to keep the Blanco from the blue serge of the uniform.

Anyway with all this pressing and cleaning I passed this inspection and along with many of my classmates we stepped 'ashore' or out of the gate as it were. We almost marched down the road not daring to saunter as even once out of sight of St Vincent we knew that in uniform we were a visual target for off duty instructors or ships company to home in on. Our best ploy would be to disappear out of sight and one of the few places was to go to the cinema. There wasn't much else to do apart from catching the ferry across to Portsmouth. We had to be mindful that arriving back at even one minute past 1900hrs would involve stoppage of future leave as well as some other punishment.

The following week on the Sunday, for some pettifogging reason, my uniform didn't pass inspection and I missed the first 'liberty boat'.

I dashed back to the accommodation block to put right whatever was wrong and dashed back to the gate only to be told the next liberty boat wasn't until 1400hrs. I stood there looking out of the gate only two steps from the freedom I had waited all week for. I bit my lip, turned on my heel and doubled back to the block (we weren't allowed to walk) from where I thought I had escaped if only for a few hours. The unfairness of it all welled up inside me. Determined not to give them the chance to inspect and reject me again I hung up my uniform for another week, got out a book, climbed to the platform of the mast and tried to lose myself in another world. The whole thing seemed a sick joke, but as the lads would say, "If you can't take a joke you shouldn't have joined".

Survival of the fittest

When I look at my service documents I can see that on entry as a fifteen year old boy my stature was measured as five feet and one half inch and that my chest measurement was twenty nine inches. Not very large by today's standard but then post war a lot of us boys were quite scrawny as we hadn't lived on the fat of the land, most things being dictated by the ration book and in our family lack of money. I overheard a couple of lads from my class saying how much money they had saved up in their money boxes at home. In our house what we called the 'money box' was the coin fed electric meter by the front door. It had two slots, but I can only ever remember feeding pennies into the larger slot to enable us to hear the rest of "Dick Barton – Special Agent", our favourite radio programme, never a silver shilling coin into the smaller slot. When dad's ship was sunk, his pay from the shipping company ceased immediately, along with mum's meagre allowance. Being prior to the days of the modern benefit system, this was a particularly hard time. We lived on a council estate amongst people who in the main were the very salt of the earth. We were blessed with some kind neighbours. Before breakfast and school us boys would take our turn to go round to one of them to borrow perhaps a cup of sugar, half a loaf or sometimes a couple of pennies with which to feed our money box. The ones we could borrow from, the most generous, were the ones also struggling to survive.

Luckily our father was a lifetime member of the Chadwell Working Men's Club whose fortnightly concerts were a highlight for us. Their annual day trip to Walton-on-the-Naze or to Southend or Maldon, just a few miles along the road in Essex, were our only window to the outside world and we found it exciting to be in a procession of motor coaches.

The three of us elder boys leaving home was a help to the family budget and with sleeping space. It hadn't mattered during the day and evening time as when not at school we would be outdoors.

The Navy fed me and over-clothed me. I learned how to survive and hold my ground, both as a class member of about twenty five boys and from close scrutiny by instructors whose harsh and unbending standards would either make or break us. Most of us survived the year of our training although some were back classed until they fitted the mould. The 'tallest on the flanks, shortest in the centre' method of forming a drill squad had suited me, being one of the shortest in stature, I could bury myself in the midst of the pack. Standing closest to the awkward lad, the one who would swing both arms forward as he stepped off to march, or one that resembled a bag of rags however hard he tried to look smart, was another tactic I learned, as they would absorb much of the flak that the drill instructor fired off.

As we moved about as a squad between the various instruction activities at the double march, spent time in the gym, at gun drill, boat pulling, as well as sporting activities and cross country runs, we increased our fitness levels.

My next entry of personal description notes that at age eighteen my stature was five foot nine and that my chest measured thirty six inches. The strange thing is my eye colouring had changed from green to blue and my complexion from 'fresh' to 'fair'.

Nearing the end of our time at St Vincent we looked forward to receiving our postings. I had seen the classes ahead of us being sent perhaps to an aircraft carrier, some to 'Vanguard' the only remaining battleship or to a destroyer or frigate. I hoped to go to one of the smaller warships, a destroyer or frigate but when my posting was to a cruiser, the 'Superb' at Chatham, I wasn't disappointed in fact I was quite pleased as having been aboard her at 'Navy Days' she struck me as being efficient and smart, quite superb.

PART 2

HMS Superb
East Indies Fleet

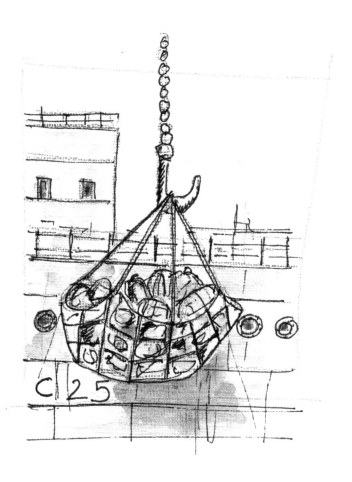

The last of The Minotaurs

I joined the 'Superb' (or Super 'B' as we came to know her) in Chatham dockyard with a group of other lads from my class at St Vincent. She was the last of the Minotaur class light cruisers although slightly different to her predecessors, one of which was 'Swiftsure', another Chatham based ship. I had been aboard both of these ships some years earlier during 'Navy Days'.

Superb looked different now, as we threw down our large kit bags and hammocks from the back of the R.N. truck that had collected us from Chatham station. All was hustle and bustle with stores being hoisted aboard from stocks piled high on the jetty. She had tenders alongside supplying fresh water and other stores and numerous cables and hoses led from the jetty to the upper deck and the interior of the ship.

We were about to struggle up the steep gangway with our bulky kit when a large bearded leading stoker shouted down from where he was leaning on the upper deck guardrail. "Take them down level with the boat deck and I'll hoist them aboard with the crane" he said. Apart from his kindly intervention we had been completely ignored.

Later that afternoon we assembled around our messdeck tables, two decks below the upper deck, close to the steering position. Our divisional officer, a Lieutenant Commander of the Royal Australian Navy introduced himself and his Lieutenant No. 2. He told us that the Superb's captain was the 5th Earl of Cairns, whose previous command had been the boys' training establishment HMS Ganges – similar to St Vincent but even bigger. The Honorable Earl, it seems, was determined that Superb's Boys Division would prove the effectiveness of training systems that he had introduced. We would be grist to the mill.

Our antipodean divisional officer gave me the impression that he was destined for greater things and we were merely stepping stones to help him on his journey. Luckily for us, the deputy divisional officer was a kindly, thoughtful and effective example to us, even though he was usually swimming against the tide of apathy generated from above.

My abiding memory of Lt. Anderson, he was officer of the day on the quarterdeck dressed in his immaculate whites, telescope under his arm, I was returning from ashore with some other lads in the put-put boat (as we called the small dhow-like craft the ship chartered to take liberty men to and fro). I had taken over the tiller from the Arab master. I performed a few pirouettes at speed before cutting the engine and gliding it alongside the platform of the accommodation ladder. Lieutenant Anderson, bless him, was bouncing up and down with pleasure and congratulated me on my performance. Many other officers would have taken a dim view, but not he.

"How did you manage that?" asked Driscoll. "By guess and by God" I answered "It just happened right. Remember how I used to crunch the motor cutter at St Vincent". "That's why I was ready to jump overboard. Bloody good job Anderson was O.O.D." Driscoll replied.

That little episode took place in the harbour of Zanzibar island off the Kenyan coast. Whenever my wife uses cloves to spice the food she is cooking the aroma transports me back in time to Zanzibar the Spice Island and to Lieutenant Anderson.

We lived and Worked
Cheek by Jowl

Superb had a crew of over 850 souls, more when we had the Admiral and his staff aboard and even more when the Royal Marine band came with him.

I probably never clapped eyes on at least half of the crew and I don't suppose I knew a quarter of them by sight, many less of them by name. You must bear in mind that most of the crew were divided into four watches, others into three watches and some were day workers.

When not on watch most of the seamen were employed in one of three parts of ship and these would also be their stations for entering and leaving harbour. Those of the forecastle were responsible for the anchors and cables and forrard moorings. The topmen for the boats, the booms, the Jacobs ladders and fenders, the mast and forward funnel. The quarterdeck for the after funnel, stern moorings and towing arrangements, for the gangway and accommodation ladders and for the quarterdeck and its awnings. The seamen's action stations would be close to their respective parts of ship.

I was a topman for the whole of the commission so I worked mainly with the same group of people. The mechanical engineers and engine room articifers worked mainly below decks in the boiler rooms, engine room and machinery spaces. The marines lived and worked aft, manned after armament and provided guards for the gangways and the jetty as well as for the Admiral's and the Captain's quarters, the pistols cabinet and the cells.

The electrical department had their own organisation and particular areas of work. There were also ordnance articifers, shipwrights, sailmakers and even a shoe repairer, all with their own workshops. The Sick Bay had a full medical staff, attendants, surgeons and dentist. We had schoolmasters, paymasters, supply and secretarial staff, in short we had butchers, bakers, but no candlestick makers. A Chinese laundry crew who worked miracles as we would come off shore in the early hours, our tropical whites the worse for wear. The laundry's express service would have them pristine and pressed ready for our next foray ashore that evening. We also carried a Somali deck crew who would cheerfully do the most menial task in the hottest of temperatures. They set up camp in one of the passageways and in the evening would group around their hubble bubble pipes.

The ship's chapel was one of the few places of peace and calm on the ship. The chaplain, or sky pilot as we called him, was one of the few people anyone with troubles could unburden to. Apart from Sunday and other church services he was called on to conduct a burial at sea for one of the articifers who died of natural causes. The body was sewn into a weighted canvas bag by the sailmaker. The ship was stopped and silent for the moving service, the traditional three volleys of musketry were fired by the marine honour guard, the bugler played the Last Post as the white ensign covered body was committed to the deep.

The ship was divided into numerous watertight compartments, some with armoured hatches and some with airlock doors. Down below it could be hot and airless, ventilation systems just pushing hot air about.

Two thirds of the ship were 'no go' areas except for those whose duty took them there. There were separate messes and messdecks for different departments and unless invited, there was little social interaction between the various messes.

We lived, ate and slept on our crowded messdeck with only a couple of feet between the hammocks when they were slung. During the daytime the hammocks had to be lashed up and stowed in nettings around the ship's side. It was called broadside messing, the food being collected from the ship's galley to be served on our scrubbed wooden mess-table. The more modern cafeteria system, with a dining hall close to where the food was cooked, had not yet reached this part of the Navy.

What with all the oil fuel, the cordite, artillery shells, gun ammunition, pyrotechnics, the warheads for torpedoes and other inflammable stores in the tanks and magazines below our feet, it was obvious we took firefighting and damage control very seriously. We of course trained for all eventualities.

Atomic, biological and chemical warfare was a real threat during the cold war years – probably still is really. We had to be able to shut the ship down and operate from a citadel below decks.

During states of alert we would have a wash down system rigged with dozens of hoses projecting a continuous curtain of spray for the ship to steam through. Its purpose was to wash any radioactive fallout from all upper surfaces of the ship. Modern ships have these systems inbuilt.

To sum up, there were few home comforts and not at all like being on daddy's yacht – if only he had one.

I spent 18 months on the ship, we lived and worked cheek by jowl and yet from the date of my next posting I never saw one of them again.

59

We lived and worked
cheek by jowl

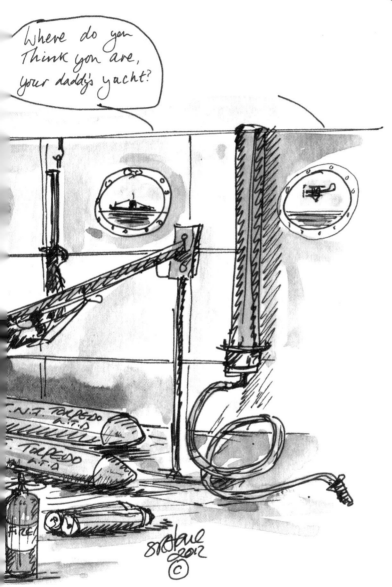

Pipe down and speak up

There were two or three ex-Arethusa boys at St Vincent during my time there, one of whom was in my class. T.S. Arethusa, formerly named 'Peking' a 'Pamir' class flying P', as they were known, was built during 1911 in Germany. She was a wood built three master, in use as a training ship for boys from disadvantaged backgrounds since 1933 and was a part of the Shaftesbury Homes charitable organisation which was formed in 1834. The products of Arethusa were well trained boys, respected and having a head start in most areas of seamanship. Many of them went on to have successful careers in the R.N, the R.F.A, or the Merchant Marine.

As I remember, most of us boy seamen didn't know much about the background and home life of the other boys in our class. Many of them I thought came from more refined or advantaged backgrounds than mine as they found the discipline meted out harsh. I found it tolerable as I don't think I was picked on without reason and looking back I can only hope that others weren't either.

'Stan' was the ex-Arethusa boy in our class and was the only boy with whom I went into any depth about my childhood – not because he was a particular friend but once he knew I came from a large family he used to ask me about my brothers and sisters and our life and the things we got up to. He came with me to the Superb, to Chatham a couple of miles from his former home the Arethusa, which was moored at Upnor, up river from the dockyard.

Upon leaving the dockyard the ship moved up to Sheerness to ammunition ship. Here we took on ammo via cranes on the jetty and from ammunition lighters moored alongside us. I didn't realise how much, either in tonnage or type, we needed to store on board. I won't bore you with the details, suffice to say it was long hours and hard work. I can't recall the ship's itinerary, but I know we paid a visit to Shotley Gate, the site of HMS Ganges, our Captain's previous command, that wasn't long before our departure to the East Indies.

I think the original plan was to call at Gibraltar for a few days before heading to Malta where the ship and its crew would carry out its 'work up' which would test ours and the ship's proficiency to carry out whatever might be demanded during the commission. I'm not sure when the plan changed, but all of a sudden we put on speed as we crossed the Bay of Biscay, our bow like a knife through butter throwing up spray as far aft as the bridge. We would still call in at Gib, but Malta and 'work up' was out of the window, or in naval parlance out of the scuttle, though ours were shut and clipped, deadlights down.

I think it was for reasons of the weather up top, stopping us from doing our usual work, we had a couple of days where we were granted 'make and mend' which was basically a half day off, supposedly to maintain our uniforms, but boys being boys, anytime we chanced to sit down we fell asleep.

I've gone round the world a bit to explain why after 'pipe down' we weren't tired enough to sleep the sleep of the knackered. Once the duty boys' instructor had been through to check we were all turned in with lights out, Stan started to ask questions about my home life. Talking quietly I told him that like him I was born at the start of the war and although I had a father I never saw him much until I was over three years old, as he was away in the Merchant Navy, until his ship the S.S. Quebec City was sunk in the South Atlantic.

I was the third born, two elder brothers and one younger, not much more than a year to eighteen months between each of us. Three years later our sister, Eileen, was born, then after another two years, along came another brother, Dave. A rest for mum of four years before Kassy (Kathleen) came on the scene and two years later our brother Terry was born. Unfortunately, Terry had a heart defect, spending months in hospital before dying at home as a baby. It was a very sad time for us all, but ten times harder for Mum, she had tried everything to give Terry the best chance. Eight children in about sixteen years without neglecting one of us, our dear Mum had her hands full and an empty purse always – I never heard her complain or lose her cool. She loved us all equally and that's all we needed.

Us four elder boys, being closer in age, were free to roam. It was pretty safe to do so in those days in our village. The war was close as we lived high above Tilbury with its docks and shipping targets. The German bombers would follow the Thames, which glistened in the moonlight, to reach London. Some would bomb targets of opportunity or strategic importance on their way – like Tilbury. On occasion our quiet village would get the benefit of poorly aimed bombs. One in our neighbour's shed and one down the chimney of the house at the bottom of our garden. Being incendiaries the resulting fires had to be doused. The next day half the village were out in the lucerne field digging up these incendiary bombs to keep as souvenirs. Health and safety had a low priority in those days.

Our position overlooking Tilbury was an ideal sighting for the AA guns, which would blaze away at the incoming bombers, as we huddled under the table or down in the corrugated iron, earth covered Anderson shelter in the back garden.

There was a massive explosion one night as a parachute delivered land mine exploded in the woods leaving a large crater which eventually turned itself into a pond, a home for wildlife a gift of nature from Hitler.

The guns were sited the far side of our playing field on one side of the woods. The other side of the woods was our playground. We had names for most of its prominent trees and pathways. (I guarantee there are many men of that locality, like me now in their seventies, who like us and perhaps with us, roamed the woods and climbed the trees, would still remember the 'entrance tree', a large elm, and the 'armchair tree' a large gnarled oak.)

I thought that only Stan was listening to me, but soon other boys were chipping in. One of the boys from Tilbury spoke about the bombing they suffered. Another boy from the east end of London, his voice quaking with emotion told us of the devastation his street suffered and the loss of two of his cousins.

To try and lighten the mood, I told them about the Spitfire that landed on our playing field but as soon as our local bobby came peddling and puffing along on his old upright bike, the pilot gunned the engine, trundled the Spit over the rough grass and took off in the direction from which he had arrived, leaving us gang of urchins waving and cheering in his prop wash. My eldest brother, Ken, who knew most things, told us he was the son of Mrs Moynihan, a nice lady who lived down our road.

One day we watched as a Mosquito twin engined fighter, the fastest
plane the Air Force had, chased after a Doodlebug flying bomb, trying
to shoot it down.

Shortly after 'D' Day, the 6th June 1944, we had lines of tanks parked
along the main road, waiting to clank down the hill to the docks to be
loaded and shipped to the Mulberry harbours at the Normandy beaches.
We would cadge chewing gum from the Canadian soldiers and pick up
tank grease which we used as plasticine for modelling.

Shortly after the war, a field hospital camped on our back field. The
soldiers would give us rides in their jeeps and trucks. For some reason
one of the soldiers threw a can of petrol over one of my brothers. He

came home reeking, luckily for the soldier our dad was away, but even so our granddad, our mother's dad, was living with us. Although a mild mannered man, he stormed over to find the commanding officer to tear him off a strip and got him to punish the culprit.

One of the boys from Tilbury said they used to come up as a gang to raid us, which I remembered. Silly as it might sound nowadays, all us boys would carry catapults which we made ourselves. The shops condoned it, by stocking catapult elastic, which is what you would ask the shopkeeper for. We fired stones at targets and I'm ashamed to say, at birds as well, but I don't think we hit many. During our raids with the Tilbury-ites, or the Orsett-ites, we carried a stock of crab apples, but even those were pretty lethal. In the winter time most of us boys would carry 'winter warmers'. These were tins punctured with nail holes and suspended from a wire loop handle. The tin would be stuffed with paper, wood and coal chippings. Once lit, we would swing it around by the handle to get the coal glowing hot. There was plenty of coal chippings to be had, as every house fire burned it, as did the steam trains as well as the traction engines that ploughed the fields. We would keep our winter warmers alight most of the day, until as often happened the wire handle broke or the tin burned through. We probably got more warmth from swinging it about than from the coal itself, but they kept us busy and amused.

After a while I could hear some of the boys knocking out Z's and I guessed I'd bored them into unconsciousness, but the very next night Stan and another boy were prompting me about the school I had attended.

Well, I was four when I started school, the local primary. The war was almost over but my two brothers used to tell me that if the air raid siren sounded on our way to school we would run back home to the Anderson shelter in our back garden, not to the big concrete shelter at the school. My eldest brother, Ken, had done well at the school. Not so well had Johnny done, he was more easy going, happy go lucky and a joker. He was a promising goal keeper and the champion 'ditch hopper' while at senior school. (The ditches on Tilbury marsh, close to St Chads School, were a challenge for the boys to jump. John excelled but didn't always make it all the way across and would often go back into school after dinner break muddy and soaking.)

I went on to become boys captain at the junior school, but I think after six months they must have reconsidered their options because it was decided the captaincy would be in periods of six month only, to give other boys a chance.

My younger brother, Mick, the fourth musketeer, was one of the few in each year to pass the eleven plus exam and go on to the grammar school. We were pleased as it put a few of the pushy parents noses out of joint, but I think it gave our mum another headache trying to keep up with the uniform demands. Us lesser mortals at the secondary school got away with 'hand me downs', far more comfortable and expendable.

I was a bookworm at school, while Mick was reading Latin and history, I was reading Biggles. At senior school I was head librarian, it was akin to putting a chocoholic in charge of the sweet shop. Reading of Columbus, De Gama and the likes of Mercator widened my horizons, taught me some geography and re-enforced my thoughts of joining the Navy.

Stan would ask me about my dad who I told him we called 'Jake' after the Daily Mirror's 'Life with the Ruggles' cartoon character. I told him I never really had any conversation with him until I was much older and he was much calmer. I said that Dad was from a large Irish family. His father had been away at the front during the first world war but after returning home he had fallen foul of two military policemen on Purfleet station, probably because he should have been in barracks. Anyway, it seems that the M.P's came off second best and grandad was on the run, living in Liverpool as a Doyle (his mother's maiden name) until after the war was long over.

Dad (Jake) became a bit of a handful, so much so, that the local priest took him to a Captain Tubbs of the Atlantic Transport Line who lived in Grays. In pretty short order Jake became a deck boy aboard S.S. Minnetonka which had been used before the war to ship cattle to and fro across the Atlantic between Britain, the U.S. and Argentina. With the war in the Dardenelles raging, the ship would pick up the artilleries horses that had crossed France by rail to Marseilles and transport them from there, by sea, to land them close to the battlefield.

It wasn't long after having disembarked the horses and other stores, that a German submarine put a torpedo or two into her. Dad told me he just had time to dash down below and rescue his mandolin, the only thing he owned of any value, before taking to the boats.

Many years later I was killing time while my wife was in the shops, flicking through books in Wickford Library when I came upon one titled: 'Silent Service, Diary of an Old Sailor' written by ordinary seaman Bill Brandon, detailing his service aboard HMS Rifleman, a torpedo boat destroyer. It was written in diary form. The page opened at 30th January 1918, the entry read: '1500hrs, as duty destroyer at Malta we got orders to put to sea at once to rescue survivors of S.S. Minnetonka in company with HMS Sheldrake'.

Regarding S.S. Quebec City on Saturday 19 September 1942 while on passage from Cape Town to Freetown, Sierra Leone the ship was torpedoed by the German submarine U-156 under the command of Captain Hartenstein, a very humane man. The U-boat surfaced and its captain instructed his men to help the survivors and showed them charts and the course to steer for the nearest land. They were 900 miles south west of Sierra Leone.

There were two packed lifeboats of survivors. The one containing my father was 12 days sailing toward land when they were rescued by the Navy. I have in my possession a book titled 'The Enemy We Killed, My Friend'. It was written by David C. Jones who served as a cadet aboard Quebec City. He was in the second of the lifeboats which reached land after 14 days.

U-156 was sunk 8 February 1943 its crew were all lost. The ship it had sunk prior to Quebec City was the liner 'Laconia' which apart from its crew and other passengers had 1,500 Italian prisoners aboard. A controversial story too long to tell here.

Boom Time, dream time
and breakfast time

It was tradition in the Andrew for boy seamen to be called an hour before the rest of the crew when the ship was in harbour. Their lordships obviously thought we needed less sleep. We all had different things to clean or polish. 'Brightwork' springs to mind which in the main to the Navy would mean brass. In the officers' mess it would be silver but that would be cleaned by wardroom stewards. Most of our brightwork would be on upper decks and guess what, salt water and salt laden air soon reacts with brass and turns its surface green, thus we were in a continual battle with nature to keep shiny the brass plates, the bell, hand rails and other items that more enlightened Navies like the Yanks would have chrome plated.

My daily task as a topman was to scrub the port boom, I think it was more symbolic than necessary, as it never really got dirty as such, just salt encrusted like most things above decks. It was another thing that made one's ship look efficient and smart especially if viewed from any Pompey or Guzz ship that might be at anchor nearby, they were always running to keep up, even when we were only marking time. Even though we were 'Chatham gentlemen' we would taunt the boy seamen from those of ships of the lower order.

The boom itself was a heavy timber spar about 30ft in length, from memory. One of these was fitted either side of the ship about six feet down from the upper deck just forward of the boat deck which was amidships between the two funnels. Stowed on the boat deck when we were at sea were the ship's boats. The 36ft pinnace crewed by Royal Marines was used for any heavy work to transfer equipment or stores and could embark over 50 passengers, ideal for putting landing parties ashore or liberty men if shore based MFV's (motor fishing vessels) were not available. The Navy had many of these not for fishing as the name implies but for use outside of sheltered waters. The 32ft motor cutter was the general workhorse, not a fast boat, about 7 knots, but like boy seamen useful. She could carry up to 30 liberty men packed tight, or less when they came off shore prostrate. More glamorous were the hard chine boats, the Captain's fast motor boat, a 35 footer, she could plane at over 16 knots with her twin throttles wide open and what we called the skimmer, only 16ft in length, she could bounce along at a similar speed.

If we were to be at sea for a long period, or expecting seas to be rough even on a short trip, the booms would be unshackled from their swivel mountings on the inboard ends and hoisted inboard for secure stowage. In situations other than this the boom would be swiveled to face aft, its outboard end would fit in a crutch affixed to the ship's side. When we entered harbour to anchor, or to moor to buoys, both booms would be swung out but of course if we went alongside a jetty, only the boom outboard could be used. My job would be to clamber over the port guardrail and down the steps welded to the steel plates of the ship's side to shackle the topping lift and the fore and aft guys to the ringbolts on the spider band of the boom.

I would of course be tended on a lifeline fixed by a bowline around my waist, which I tied myself as was my custom, having seen some of the granny knots our few national servicemen would tie. You must bear in mind that the ship would still be under way, preparing to enter harbour and could be making anything up to 15 knots. When we eventually dropped anchor at the same instant the ensign would be struck from the after mast and replaced by one at the stern and the Jack, the union flag, raised at the Jackstaff at the point of the bow. The booms would be swung out and be secured square and horizontal to the ship. Within short order the ship's boats would be slung and lifted out by the crane, to be secured to the lizards of the booms, the lighter boats outboard. Myself and other boys from the top division would have rigged these securing lizards and the Jacob's ladders, which the boat's crews used to man or to leave their boats by. Any passengers would embark or disembark using the accommodation ladders at the quarterdeck.

As I have said before my daily task involved balancing while clutching my bucket of hot water and scrubber with one hand and the wire rope of the topping lift with the other as I made my way to the outboard end where I would sit astride the boom and scrub my way backwards toward the ship's side. There were associated hazards with this task, firstly as the boom was about seven feet or so above the water below and the prevailing wind or tide could push the bows of the boats which were secured to the boom forward and be immediately below the scrubber scrubbing, falling into or onto one of them could be more than just painful.

Falling into the water was not a hazard in itself but falling amongst some of the sea's unfriendly inmates could be. A number of times especially at ports around the Red Sea and Gulf of Aden, I had seen hungry looking sharks, lean mean killing machines, licking their lips, hoping for a tasty morsel to fall out of the sky or off the boom. Sometimes

I would see the triangular shapes of some kind of rays amongst the sharks. I thought most types were bottom feeders, but these and the sharks seemed to know mealtimes aboard the ship and would gather around the gash (waste food) chute, which was rigged to enable the food waste to enter the sea without spoiling our gleaming grey paint job that we applied so lovingly. I think these creatures had learned the meaning of the bugle calls 'Cooks to the galley' and 'Hands to breakfast', or dinner, or whatever.

It didn't take me long to realise that neither the buffer (Chief Boatswain's Mate) nor the top division P.O. ever actually inspected the boom, as it would mean coming out onto the boom itself, which they wouldn't have done since being boy seamen themselves or even had never done since during the war years the Jerries couldn't care less if your booms were clean or dirty. They were happy just as long as I was out there. If I finished early they had the problem of finding me another, sometimes pointless, task to do. So I would take my time and gaze into the clear blue water below me and dream of becoming a Jacques Cousteau cum Don Winslow diver explorer. 'Buster' Crabbe, the well-known Royal Navy frogman (Commander Lionel Crabbe OBE GM RN) had been in the news having disappeared while carrying out espionage on Sverdlov class cruisers of the Soviet Navy during their visit to Portsmouth. His body had not at that time been found. With all this in mind and having watched our ship's diving team in action I requested to go on a shallow water diving course as soon as I became 18 years old, which was the age requirement.

Little did I realize as I sweltered and basked in the sun that the combination of time passing and bureaucratic cogs turning, resulted in me reporting to HMS Safeguard the boom defence base and diving school at North Queensferry, Fife, just under the Forth railway bridge and close to Rosyth dockyard where unbeknown to me then, I would join my first submarine where she was being refitted. Happy days, it was mid-winter and freezing. Unlike the aqua-lung equipment Jacques Cousteau was helping to develop we would be using oxygen re-breather sets which were through a bag on the chest. Breathing oxygen we were limited to 32ft otherwise we would risk oxygen poisoning and mainly wearing leaden boots rather than flippers. The rubber suits were of the 'one size fits all' variety. The rubber greys to seal the suit at the wrists and the face seal didn't actually seal so the cold water soon leaked in. Diving in the mud and murk of Rosyth dockyard, trying to find the shot line that lead vertically down from the boat above, after having taken ten paces forward, ten paces left, then retrace your steps the way you thought you had come from, soon proved how disorientating things could become. Trying to cut a chain link with hammer and chisel against the shot weight, was more than just tiring, I found it nigh impossible. The hands completely unprotected would bleed if you knocked them on anything once you came to the surface – now I knew what the expression "Bleeding cold today isn't it" meant, still "If you can't take a joke you shouldn't have joined" and I had to remember I volunteered for this.

My water had started hot but was now cold and had lost any suds it had, not to worry job done time for breakfast, 'shit on a raft' I hoped. At least no boat's crew had been called to man their boat. That didn't happen too often before breakfast. It was those times before breakfast when all boy seamen were employed spreading and rigging the quarterdeck awnings or painting the ship's side from plank stages suspended from above and lowered by ourselves by easing the turns around the horn. It was better to do the painting early morning before the heat of the day.

But this did mean I would be scrubbing the boom later in the day when boat's crews would trample me to death, like a cockroach under foot – such is life.

"Do you hear there – away
Captains motor boats crew"

I don't think I've mentioned it before but all tannoy messages were preceded by the alert "Do you hear there" and woe betide any that failed to act on a message that involved them responding to it. Throughout the ship, in the mess decks, cubby holes and noisy machinery spaces there would be people asking "What was that last pipe?".

In response to this particular pipe the boat's crew would scurry to board their boat in quick time. Better to have to loiter off the ship's quarter, engine idling to await the quartermaster's arm signal to come alongside the accommodation ladder, than to keep the captain and his guests waiting on the quarterdeck.

In their haste the boat's crew wouldn't wait for me to come inboard off of the boom, they just clambered over me as I ducked down as low as I could, gripping the slippery wooden boom with the cheeks of my bum whilst clinging to my bucket and scrubber for dear life. I did not want to go through the 'lost bucket and scrubber' court marshal with the buffer (Chief Bosun's Mate – who was entrusted by their lordships with accounting for what were supposedly consumable stores.)

How I envied the boat's crew as they manned their launch, clad in white fronts, white bell-bottom trousers and plimsols. The launches, the Admiral's barge, known as the parrot because of its green and white colour and the Captain's motor boat in dark blue and white – you could see your reflection in their gloss finish – I couldn't, I only watched from above, clutching my bucket, as they swung down the Jacobs ladder, started the engine and dropped the boat astern to clear the other boats secured to the boom. I could hear her exhausts and circulating water burbling away until the coxswain pushed the throttles forward and the boat surged ahead. She soon lifted up onto her chines as she attained her planing trim.

The bow and sternsman went through a routine with their chrome ended boathooks, while the launch made a sweeping curve to gain her loitering position on the ship's quarter, to await the quartermaster's arm signal.

Those with the boathooks were fellow boy seamen. Every three months or so, the list of job changes would be posted on the Commander's office notice board.

I was eagerly anticipating either boat's crew or side boy to the quartermaster. I scanned the list for my change. I went from port boom to starboard boom. As they say, life is full of disappointments and I consoled myself that sometimes its better the devil you know.

We Were an outpost for The foreign office

Captain, the Earl of Cairns, loved to see 'his' boats creaming around the harbours of his domain, the Indian Ocean, the Red Sea and the Persian Gulf. The Navy says that 'a ship is known by her boats', ours had to be the crème de la crème. The other naval presence in the area, the Yanks, they never worried. Their boats, big, heavy, noisy diesels, would jockey about, gunning their engines, to-ing and fro-ing to come alongside. It pleased the Right Honorable Captain to send a launch to bring important guests aboard – Arab sheiks, princes, diplomats, consuls – we were an outpost for the Foreign Office. They could have driven up the jetty in a car, but far better the boat's crew trample me half to death, while I tried to scrub the boom. After dark the ship would be floodlit. Guests would arrive by launch so they could ascend the accommodation ladder to be met on the spotless, scrubbed quarterdeck by the sword toting, white doughboy clad, welcoming party and the Royal Marine guard, (turkeys we called them, but never to their faces, as we had some of the toughest marines ever invented). The Royal Marine Band, if we had the Admiral on board, the white jacketed stewards proffering cocktails from their silver trays, the whole ambience, the cocktail party under quarterdeck awnings was the next best thing to being at a Buckingham Palace garden party. Not that I had been to either, but I had scrubbed the white planked wood of the quarterdeck many a time.

After retiring from the Navy, the Earl of Cairns served as Marshal of the Diplomatic Corps.

A great Sporting event

One typical Indian Ocean day, sunny and blue, I learnt that the captain had caught a swordfish and that it was now hanging from one of the gun barrels of 'Y' turret, the triple barreled 6" at the quarterdeck. A rare event for us, the great unwashed, as we were allowed to marvel at the fruits of this great sporting event from the hallowed ground of the quarterdeck, which we kept so beautifully scrubbed and clean. It was a sport reserved for our only blueblood, the 5th Earl. To me it was a melancholy sight.... like a fish out of water. It was 'caught' by the sharp end of a .303 bullet, then 'landed' by sending the seaboat to tow it alongside before hoisting it inboard. I was interested to see such an animal, the only swordfish I have ever actually seen. It must have measured about twelve feet from sword to tail and weighed about 10cwt. It seemed even less sporting to me than tricking it to swallow a hook with the deception of a tasty piece of squid on it, but then what do we mere plebs know of such things. All I did know was that swordfish steaks did not travel as far down the food chain as the boy seaman's mess. Too rich for our palettes I assumed.

A swordfish is one of the fastest fish. They normally swim at about 500ft, but often bask on the surface, airing their dorsal fin – making them an easy target.

Christmas 1956

I think this was the worst Christmas I had spent, mind you I was only 17. We were at anchor at Trincomalee. I spent part of the morning delivering messages of goodwill from one officer to another, knocking at cabin doors to pass these messages of good cheer and sometimes some silly gift. I wondered what my family at home were doing, pound to a pinch of snuff, whatever they were doing it would have been a lot more sincere and heartfelt than what was going on here. It didn't feel like Christmas because of the heat and sunshine, but at least today I wasn't up so early to scrub the boom. I couldn't knock the effort put in by the catering branch, the food was good all day, but even that did little to lift my mood.

I could hear the motor boat's engine as it roared away from (my) starboard boom. I recognized its engine to be that of the captain's motor boat, but didn't recall hearing the tannoy message calling the crew away and didn't expect to, as to my knowledge the crew were stood down for the day. I knew that because one of her crew was a fellow boy seaman from the top division.

I heard an amplified voice shouting through a hand held megaphone so I moved from where I was leaning on to the port guardrail abreast of 'B' turret, to the starboard side and moved aft to the boat deck. I could see the motor boat lifting up to plane on her hard chine as she accelerated away. The strange thing was, instead of her normal four man crew, I could only see the coxswain. I recognized him immediately to be leading seaman Jesse Tonks. Jesse was without a doubt the most skilful of the boat coxswains, even better than the admiral's barge coxswain.

The boat was a twin screw fast motor boat and could reach a top speed

of about 16 knots on the smooth surface of the sheltered anchorage. As I moved further aft I recognized the irate voice coming through the megaphone to be none other than that of our esteemed Australian divisional officer. The motor boat having left turning screws, began to describe anti-clockwise circles around the ship.

Our blond, suntanned, Lieutenant Commander was turning white with rage to have his strident orders ignored. He was after all a gunnery officer, a product of Whale Island, Portsmouth – as such it was akin to ignoring the Lord almighty. In the end, even with his thick skin, he began to realize how silly it was making threats, as Jesse had no intention of bringing the boat back.

It was the fastest boat we had so there was nothing to do but wait for Tonks to relent or run out of fuel and eventually it was the latter that resolved the issue. The boat was towed back by the seaboat, Jesse was confined to a cell until after New Year's Day. When he came out he was an ex-leading seaman and no longer coxswain of the captain's motor boat.

Jesse certainly livened up an otherwise dull day, perhaps that was his intention.

Diyata Lawa

The R.N. had more 'pussers red devils' than it had ships. No doubt somewhere in Whitehall there was an admiral and staff responsible for them. I have seen them in training bases, oiling stations, naval barracks, dockyards, all points of the compass, anywhere that the white ensign flies. If only they could all be mustered together, have all the ships at Spithead and all the 'red devils' on Southsea common. That would scupper the Yanks.

Just to explain, what we called the red devil was the Andrews equivalent of the posties bike, a status symbol for an officer to have one of his own. (In Nelson's day he probably rode a white charger). On a shore base the Regulating Office had one, the buffer had two or three, anybody and everybody's messenger had one to clank about on. Here at Diyatalawa were about twenty of them, a whole squadron in fact.

Our base in Ceylon was the beautiful bay at Trincomalee where the

Sunderland flying boats of the RAF still touched down on its aquamarine surface, the silver sand and palm trees forming a magical backdrop. I would never then have imagined that this tranquil island would be scarred by many years of ethnic conflict and suffer the horrific tsunami.

During the summer months it was hot, searingly hot, aboard the ship stifling. Okay at sea with a breeze blowing over the deck, wind scoops out of open scuttles, camp beds set up to sleep on deck. Us boy seamen used the port and starboard tube spaces (which house the triple launching tubes for torpedoes). At our moorings at Trincomalee we sweltered.

At about 5,000ft altitude in the central highlands was the Diyatalawa rest camp, established I think during the Far East campaign of the Second World War. Vast fleets passed through Trincomalee to help push the Japanese back to their homeland and eventual defeat.

It was toward the rest camp that an R.N. bus, full of boy seamen on a two week break, wound its way up narrow roads through lush vegetation and forest. Now and again we would pass huge Indian elephants hauling logs on chains, a tiny mahout perched high on their backs. The bus, a new Bedford in its dark blue R.N. colours, exactly the same as those in Chatham barracks and elsewhere, but here it seemed huge and wide as it negotiated the mountain bends. At first we doubted the native Sinhalese driver but we soon recognized him to be an expert.

Eventually we reached the rest camp sited on a plateau, a clearing amid the greenery, with large wood built colonial style buildings, dormitories, games room, club house, shower rooms, cookhouse and dining hall. It was cool, heavenly cool. It was quiet after the constant noise of machinery and hum of motors, the bugle calls and pipes over the tannoy and the motion of the ship.

Here there was only the hum of insects, the chirping of crickets and unfamiliar calls and songs of tropical birds. I would walk for miles exploring this strange and interesting world. I had only known our local woods and Essex countryside before. I remember one day that I chanced upon a Buddhist temple. Inside were monks in saffron robes, the aroma of burning incense and a large statue of Buddha.

Let's rewind back to the red devils and my abiding memory of the stay at Diyatalawa. We used to ride these bikes around the camp most days. One beautiful day about a dozen of us set out on a jaunt. Now these bikes, as I remember, had few gears and ineffective rod linkage brakes. They had to be pushed uphill and were virtually impossible to control going down, nor able to stop short in an emergency.

After an uphill slog pushing our bikes we breasted the summit, mounted our bikes and set off down an increasingly steep twisting mountain road. I was amongst the leaders, trying to overtake a namesake of mine,

Clark (no 'e' on the end). He lived at Tilbury, a few miles from my Essex home.

Suddenly, as we rounded a sharp bend we saw in front of us a squad of Ceylonese soldiers from the local garrison, marching up the hill. How we missed them I don't know, we somehow passed between them and the verge. Behind us, just about to round the bend, were around another ten or so novice cyclists riding bikes that couldn't be stopped. Once I established some control of my mount and hearing shouts of alarm from behind, I glanced over my shoulder to see khaki clad figures scattered over the road and in the storm ditches on either side of the road.

The scene has been etched in my memory bank for over fifty years. Apart from the torrent of abuse and much shaking of fists, nobody suffered anything more than cuts and bruises. Before we got back to the camp, news of the incident had preceded us. No longer could we take the red devils out of camp.   Our divisional officer was even tougher on us when we got back to the ship.

Regarding pussers red devils, it seems they were not always painted red, just in case some officionardo smart arse is pedantic enough to challenge me with regard to the colour of those based at Diyatalawa or elsewhere. Red devils come in other colours and I think the flotilla based at Diyatalawa were actually black, because I saw a photo of one on the internet being ridden there and it was a darker shade of black. Whatever the colour, the braking system was the same – useless.

Had a good day at The laundry dear?

It was a wonderful feeling of freedom for me as a boy not yet seventeen, after being cooped up aboard the crowded, noisy ship of war to be here, walking in the cooler highlands surrounding the rest camp at Diyatalawa. I had tasted pineapple from a tin, but to be able to pluck one fresh from the plant, skin and eat it, was a new experience.

Another experience this particular day, as I climbed down the rocky bank to enable me to cross the shallow river, I came upon what I assumed was a laundry crew. A line of young women were spread out along the far bank all clad in colourful saris. Each had a pile of clothing which they were soaping, then they beat each item against the half submerged rocks, before rinsing it in the rock pools. Washed clothes had been spread out over low bushes to dry in the heat of the sun. Standing behind the girls at the centre of the line was a youngish man who watched me as I climbed down over the rocks.

The washing, beating and rinsing seemed to be on hold, the gaze of a dozen dark eyed beauties was on me. Using rocks as stepping stones, I started to pick my way across the slow flowing river. About half way over as I reached a flat rock slab, the overseer called out to me "Jig, jig master, 10 rupees". Now my naval training thus far had ruled against me being taken by surprise and had re-enforced the need for making quick decisions. You can't write home and ask your mum and dad, the GI had said.

I looked along the line, their eyes seemed to be pleading 'pick me, pick me', even if only to alleviate the boring routine of the daily wash. None had averted their eyes as many Asian women did.

The reputation of the British Navy could be at stake, it had been built up over hundreds of years and was in danger of being shattered by my decision and performance. I think I made a wise choice and had to disappoint eleven of them.

I have often wondered since what was her reply to husband or boyfriend to the question posed above.

It was not a matter of paying for sex, although I suppose we men always pay one way or another. I don't suppose she got a share of the money, it was more to compensate for the loss of a laundrywoman for half an hour.

I found the Ceylonese a very hospitable people.

Cacophony of Sound and
the Chicago Piano

Like food on the supermarket shelf, ammunition stored in cooled
magazines in the bowels of the ship, has a 'use by' date. It was time
we used much of our ammo before being re-supplied. It was therefore
arranged that our anti-aircraft armament and gun crews would test their

mettle against targets towed by aircraft.

We had five twin 4" mountings with an effective range out to four miles, six single Bofors 40mm with range about two miles and four quadruple two pounder pom-pom mountings which could send a curtain of fire out to about one mile. We also had some short range twin Oerlikon guns.

I had been a loader on one of the 4" guns. The boy seamen crewed two of the midships mountings. I worked the right hand of the two guns – ideal for a left handed person. The heavy projectiles were kept in ready use lockers adjacent to the mountings, they were already fitted with the type of fuses – either air burst or proximity – that we would use on this shoot. If the base of the proji was stood on the deck its pointed nose would reach my waist.

Shooting in local control the gunlayer and aimer would line up where they wanted the shell to hit or burst, allowing deflection for speed of the target. The ammunition supplier would pass the proji so it was cradled in my right arm and leaned on my right shoulder. I would steady it with my left fist clenched against its base and using my left arm as a piston, punch the shell forward into the open breech which was designed to trip closed on contact with the base of the brass case. As soon as the breech slammed shut the gun would fire then recoil and eject the empty brass cordite case. The shell itself would be hurtling toward the target.

The slamming shut of the breech would push up on my clenched fist which I would have to withdraw smartish and have to step back and sideways with my left foot while swiveling on my right to get me clear of the recoil. Thus there were two dangers one had to avoid – the first was losing the left fist in the breech and the second was being knocked senseless by the recoiling gun. We were kitted out to avoid other hazards as we wore anti-flash gear, helmets and ear plugs.

Unlike guns sited on land we were operating from a moving platform as the ship could be rolling, or heeling over as the ship turned at speed. Seas could be breaking over the gundeck. The combination of these things sometimes made my avoidance routines difficult to achieve, so I was quite happy after about three months, when we changed around and I was moved on to one of the quadruple pom-pom mountings.

These gun mountings were universally known as Chicago pianos. Ours was sited on the port side just below the bridge level. It had an eight man crew and again my role was a loader, this time not of heavy shells but of ammo drums containing 140 of the two pounder cartridges. The guns would fire as fast as we could load them in synchronized pairs making the staccato pom-pom noise, laying a curtain of explosive bursts out to about a mile.

Each of the mountings had an ordnance articifer in attendance, as the electrical joystick control was temperamental and the ammo was prone to jamming. He was like a piano tuner. Sometimes she would only play a few bars, but today on this shoot, the Chicago piano was performing Rachmaninov's piano concertos and Winifred Atwell's 'five finger boogie' all rolled into one, allegro molto.

I fed her drum after drum. 'Dolcie' Gray, my opposite number on the other side of the mounting was matching me, drum for drum. I could see wild excitement in his eyes. I had no time to look at the target which was a towed drogue, the tug a plane of the Indian Air Force. Today we were making the drogue dance to our tune.

On a previous shoot the aim was poor, a few wild shots burst in the patch of sky that the plane was about to fly through. The usually laconic RAF pilot, sounding highly agitated, radioed "I'm towing this flaming target – not pushing it". The Gunnery Commander was beaming with delight, this shoot was his swan song as he would be leaving us on our return to Trinco'. He was due to fly back to the mecca of the gunnery world – Whale Island, Portsmouth.

Taking his place as Gunnery Commander of Superb would be our divisional officer who had won his promotion off of our broken backs. He would now be sporting scrambled egg (as we called the gold braid affixed to the peak of his officer's cap) which all officers of Commander and above wore. Lt. Anderson would take over as our Divisional Officer for the remainder of the commission.

New things would soon be afoot as shortly boy seamen would be re-designated as junior seamen. The Andrew it seems was on the threshold of the twentieth century.

Why buy a book when you can go to a library

We were making tracks, well a frothing bubbling wake anyway, our bow wave sending the flying fish gliding, skimming the calm unruffled surface. Porpoise, a whole school of them – they didn't have much to learn, showing us the way, they had built-in satnav – before our scholars even dreamt of such things – they probably learnt it from the whales who learnt it from the dinosaurs – a mammoth task.

We still relied on the charts and star maps, updated over the years, since Magellan and Mercator's day. Nonetheless, we knew where we were headed – the Seychelle Islands – we knew because we read it on the commander's office notice board.

Now I've always had an enquiring mind, must have inherited it from my ancestors who, I'm told, had crossed from France to Ireland and then from Ireland to England. I'm not sure what they were running from or whether they found what they were looking for.

The closest I could get to the bridge and the charts was the lookouts positions adjacent. Six enormous, swivel mounted, binoculars – three per side would be used to scan the horizons, the sky and the ocean, constantly, for anything man made that may have penetrated our radar's web.

My main reference point was the ship's library where I made it my business to boff up on our next port of call. I had never heard of the Seychelles then, nor probably had anyone I knew – nowadays its just another, more exotic perhaps, holiday destination.

The Seychelles are a group of 85 islands, we were headed for Mahe the largest and more specifically to the capital, Victoria. Anyway we found it without satnav and I liked what we found. I liked the palm trees and the beach with Sharky's bar on it. I liked the giant tortoises that lived only there and the slightly rude coco de mere, or love nuts as they were commonly known which, when the outer shuck was removed, looked like a maiden's buttocks. But most of all I liked the French Madagascan girl librarian I met amongst the reference books. She satisfied my desire for knowledge and was unstinting with her time, to the extent that after work she would accompany me to Sharky's bar, where I would suffer the envious gaze of my shipmates. Since those days I have lived by the motto 'why buy a book when you can go to the library', but never have I met a librarian as enchanting as Louise – try as I might.

Guns and game east Africa

Leaving the Seychelles, my heart and my tearful Louise in our wake, our speeding bow pointed westwards toward the Kenyan coastline. Without the guiding dolphins we made our landfall at Mombasa and entered Kilindini harbour, our secondary base on the East Indies station.

We rarely met up with other ships of our small fleet, of which we were the kingpin, the core and the big fist. Today we had company, the Loch Fada and the Loch Killisport. Believe it or not, they were Loch Class Frigates, a bit old fashioned like my grandmother was and like her, very straight laced and effective. One of these two ships had shot an Egyptian Mig 15 jet out of the sky, using their hand loaded, eyeball sighted, 4" q.f. (quick firing) armament. This was during the invasion fiasco to retake the Suez Canal after it had been nationalized by Egypt's President Nasser. We were on the outer fringe of this action, which was undertaken in the main by ships in the Mediterranean. It wasn't our guns that sunk the shipping that blocked the Canal's use, but whoever's it was, we were thankful. When we eventually returned to the UK it had to be via the Cape of Good Hope and Capetown itself.

Once I had seen all I wanted of Mombasa itself, which didn't take more than a day or two, along with most of the other lads, our shore time would be spent on the beautiful silver sand beaches, playing beach volley ball, swimming and relaxing. We had endured three months spent mainly at sea in hot conditions, carried out mock war games with ships of the Indian and Ceylonese Navies during what was called J.E.T. (Joint Exercises Trincomalee) as well as making our presence known around the Persian Gulf.

In my spare time on board I had been assisting the ship's photographer, a Naval Airman like all of that branch, he would produce a set of ten to twelve pictures of the places the ship visited and of any events of interest on board. In those days few of the crew would own a camera and any that did would have to take a chance on the quality of pictures printed ashore in the places we visited. I helped him in the printing of a few hundred sets of these pictures, so crew members had a record to keep or to send home to their families.

One set of onboard events was of the 'crossing the line' ceremony, another he took was an impressive set of a night shoot involving broadsides from our heavy weapons. To take these pictures our intrepid photographer had to be lashed to the jackstaff at the point of the bow. The blast and vibration of the six forward 6" guns would have catapulted him overboard otherwise. Anyway the pictures were good and he survived.

The photographer, whose name eludes me, had arranged us a week's leave and a guide, who was a former game warden, to take us through the Tsavo Game Reserve. The guide, a middle aged, thick set, South African named George, collected us from the ship and we piled our sleeping bags into the back of his battered Morris Oxford estate. Propped up against the dashboard was his rifle, with telescopic sights affixed, on which he hung his wide brimmed hat.

The sight of it was reassuring as soon we were passing through prides of lions. I'm sure the waving of the gun with floppy hat atop would frighten any king of the beasts. We passed buffalo by the herd load, rhinos by the wide berth and giraffes with their heads in the clouds. Elephants would file across the road in front of the car as we drove at night – the grey dust that they rolled in to cool down during the heat of the day gave them a ghostly appearance when seen in our dipped headlights.

We visited Mzima Springs where hippos wallowed in the mud and we camped close to the white water rapids at Lugard Falls. I say we camped, I actually slept in the back of the shooting brake, where there was just enough room to stretch out in my maggot. The other two slept under the awning George had rigged up alongside the car. We kept a fire burning all night, not for warmth, but as a deterrent to the wild animals.

Two nights we stayed at the Kibo Hotel on the slopes of Kilamanjaro and drank John Collins. While we wined and dined our ship's marines were climbing to the peak and sleeping in two man tents under the stars. Such is life.

With regard to the shooting down of the Mig 15 at Suez, I can't authenticate which ship shot it down. It may have been neither of these ships, wishful thinking or perhaps an albatross. I don't suppose the principle actor, the pilot, cared and for us it was one less rushin jet to worry about.

Haven of Peace

We had officers of the schoolmaster branch on board the ship. Amongst their other duties, they had to continue with the education of us boy seamen. We were expected to pass E.T.1 (educational test 1), which I was exempt as an advanced class boy, E.T.2 which I had by now passed and was at this stage studying various subjects in H.E.T. (higher educational tests) having already passed some. These were service equivalents of the G.C.E.exams which normal human beings took.

One of these classes was held the evening before our arrival at Dar-es-Salaam, the chief seaport of Tanganyika (now Tanzania, a United Republic, together with the Coral Islands of Zanzibar and Pemba). This was, and still is, one of the world's poorest countries not evidenced by the hustle and bustle of the busy port. We were there before it gained independence from Britain, but I don't think its people are any the richer for that.

The 'schoolie', who I took to be a man of humour, asked around the class to give examples of nocturnal activities. He singled me out, so I gave this as my example. "I dreamed I was eating Weetabix and when I woke up my mattress was gone". I wasn't original, or particularly funny, but it was the best I could think of off the cuff. He then asked me to what I attributed my fertile imagination. My answer, "Compost and chips, sir" seemed to find the limit of his humour.

Recently, green shoots of democracy had taken root in this backwater of the senior service, in the form of a catering committee, of which schoolie was the chair. The idea was to bring variety and imagination to the menu, giving more choices selected from suggestions put forward by the peons of the lower deck. One of schoolie's ideas was to aid the catering staff by providing 'volunteers' to do menial tasks thereby releasing more cooks to spoil the broth. I found myself to be among the first of these volunteers.

In company with two 'men under punishment' I spent the first two nights of our stay in the 'Haven of Peace' (which in Arabic is Dar-es-Salaam) cleaning the galley trays used for cooking, as well as scrubbing the galley floor, the whole thing took about two and a half hours, after evening meal, by which time I was dead beat. Some of those cooks must have been on a welding course, the way they managed to fix the food to the trays.

The green shoots soon withered and died and we went back to the 'get what you're given' catering style that we had become used to.

Now they say that 'the sun always shines on the righteous' but it does shine on others as well. Coming out onto 'B' gundeck after slaving in the galley 'Nutty' and I were seeking some cool air, out of the suns rays, but everywhere Nutty settled the sun would seek him out. The work wasn't so bad for him, as he was one of the two men under punishment serving their penance.

For me, as one of schooley's volunteers I was doing it for fun!! They also say that simple men are always happy, but that was not the case with Nutty, not today, not ever really. Most of the crew regarded him as a complete idiot – which he would have been if he had ducked – now he had two front teeth missing.

In this haven of peace he had started a war before even making it ashore. His idea of a joke was to try and lift the marine sentry's holstered pistol, while his back was turned. The marine in question was the ship's butcher, a huge ginger haired South African, a marine of the strike first, strike hard variety.

The Commander didn't see the joke either, and had no sympathy with Nutty's dental deficiency. As an able seaman cannot be demoted, the Commander awarded him 14 days no. 10's which was stoppage of leave and included extra work, mostly unpleasant tasks. Not so much as a punishment said the kindly Commander, more to give you space to consider your outlook on the ways of the Royal Navy. All heart, a real leader of men.

To give Nutty his due it wasn't this that he was unhappy about now as we gazed toward the town and its forbidden pleasures. Now that he had found a shady spot he was being quite profound, as we discussed the previous couple of months we had spent in the Persian Gulf – the reason we had by-passed our work up in Malta.

We had been responding to unrest, bubbling up like oil under sand. We chased around the gulf ports putting ashore landing parties, clutching shields and toting riot sticks, to quell the unrest, which evaporated only to break out elsewhere. This caused us to up sticks and move on to counter it. I think we were being given the run around. Nutty said "Mark my words, this could go on for years, if us and the Yanks could annexe the strategic areas around the Straits of Hormuz, we could control the flow of oil through it forever and most of the world would soon accept it". Looking back now, with the benefit of 20 x 20 hindsight, I don't think Nutty was far wrong.

After my two days of voluntary work I headed for the Tanganyikan highlife, leaving Nutty and his fellow offender to consider the error of their ways. Once more I was at peace with the world.

Homeward bound

On 1st April 1956 Boy Seamen had been re-designated, I had become a Junior Seaman 1st Class although old habits died hard in the Andrew and we and others still referred to us as Boy Seamen. Job changes were posted and yes I was now boats crew. Not the launch or the Captain's motor boat, nor even the sedate motor cutter. We had no skimmer anymore, the fast 16ft boat had hit a half submerged, barely floating, log, while creaming across Trinco's blue lagoon of a harbour. The boat almost took off, leaving its after end and engine astern and sinking and its leading seaman coxswain sunk.

I was now to be bowman of the starboard seaboat. Not much glamour in that, no creaming across blue lagoons, no starched white uniform or chromed-tipped boathook choreography. Not even an engine – the motor whaler had not yet been introduced – our motive power was the muscle and sinew of the five oarsmen. My only consolation was that the crew was chosen to a large extent by its coxswain, it made me feel wanted.

It seemed ironic to be changed from scrubbing the boom now that we were homeward bound, on the long haul around the Cape of Good Hope. We would only be calling at Simonstown (which was still an R.N. base although to be passed over to the South African Navy within a year),

Dakar, the main sea port of Senegal on the Cape Verde peninsula, where we would refuel and then on to Chatham. At none of these ports would we need to tether the boats at the boom.

At sea, each watch had to have a crew for both of our seaboats, at immediate readiness for any emergency such as 'man overboard' or 'aircrew rescue' (should we be firing at towed targets a little erratically). These emergencies were more likely to occur in rough weather, so that was the weather we tended to practice in.

The 27ft whaler is a fine seaboat, we had trained on it at St Vincent in the creek, which is quite different from a moving ship in rough seas. I was familiar with the Robinson disengaging gear, with the boat's falls used for lowering and raising the boat and with the radial davits and associated equipment.

The difference now was that our coxswain, a leading seaman of long experience, insisted that we should be able to set up the disengaging gear and hook up to the falls blindfolded. Years before, as a crewman himself, he had been involved in an incident where the forward falls had not been hooked on, and the seaboat, dangling from the after falls, was swamped by the forward movement of the ship, throwing most of the crew into a rough sea. By good seamanship and a speedy emergency turn by the ship's captain, the launching of the second seaboat at the right moment, coupled with a large dose of good luck, they were all picked up unharmed.

One of my duties as bowman was to remove the pin from the disengaging hook, once the weight was taken off by the midships oarsmen leaning on the 'fore and after' which linked the forward and after hooks. I would hold up the pin for the coxswain to see, the stroke oarsman would do the same with the after pin. We now awaited the order from the officer on the deck above to 'slip' which he would give once we were at the crest of a wave. On his command the coxswain would operate the release lever, we would be pulled forward by the boat rope which I would be ready to slip, once we were clear of the ship's side, or be ready to bear off from the ship's side should we not be clear. By this time the other four oarsmen would be powering us away and I would pick up the stroke with my bow oar.

We were responding to the tannoy message "For exercise, for exercise, man overboard – away starboard seaboat's crew". A yellow painted marker buoy had been tossed over the ship's side to represent the man in the water and we were being homed on to it by arm signals from the ship, although by now it was quickly receding astern of us. Once we were away from the ship the Captain turned her hard to port to take up position to the windward of the marker buoy where he could shelter it and us as we approached the buoy from its leeward side.

I concentrated on nothing but the back of the oarsman who sat on the thwart two ahead of me, he in turn would be taking his cue from the stroke oar who sat two thwarts ahead of him. It was only the cox'n who could see ahead, he would get an occasional glimpse of the buoy as it rose on the swell. The stroke oar would watch the ship and inform the cox'n of their signals.

The critical eyes of the ship were on us, this is what much of our training had been about – physical effort, seamanship and teamwork. The cox'n gave us no orders until we neared the buoy when he quietly said "Easy oars", the signal for us to slacken pace and then shortly after "Oars" and "Stand by bowman". My job was to pass a line round the buoy, which would be towed aft and hauled inboard over our quarter.

We had the Robinson gear set up and ready for hooking on as we approached the falls from aft. My first job was to pick up the boat rope and secure it through the thwarts. The method used enabled it to be slipped quickly if needs dictated. The boat rope enabled those inboard on the ship to pull us forward onto the falls. I reported to the cox'n when I had hooked on the forrard fall and only then would the after falls be hooked on.

The rest of the watch had not been idle when we were doing our thing. They were set up ready for hoisting and before long we were secured snug at the davits. Even though we were wet, cold and tired our first duty was to prepare the seaboat ready for an instant re-launch. Once the cox'n was satisfied he would report the boat's readiness status to the officer of the watch. Only then could we dry off and get a hot cup of Ki and look forward to our relief when the next watch took over.

We also used the seaboats to recover practice torpedoes. These were fitted with a blowing head rather than a warhead as (A) we didn't want to sink our own ships and (B) these torpedoes were expensive items. When the 'fish' completed its run it would float vertically in the water. We would secure its nose and run a loop over and down to its tail, then pull it up horizontal before securing it alongside the boat, ready for hoisting inboard on our return to the ship. The seaboat was also used to transfer the buoy jumper, but this did not happen during my time as boat's crew.

Without hope at Good Hope

H.M.S. Ceylon was on her way out from the U.K. She would be relieving us as flagship of the East Indies fleet. There would be no formal handover, no ceremonial passing of the baton, just ships that pass in the night.

We had been a work horse. She was more for show, having been at the Gold Coast when it became Ghana and at the independence ceremonies for Nigeria. 'Ceylon' would hand over Simonstown to the South African Navy and later Trincomalee to the Ceylonese Navy. Mind you she was a Portsmouth ship.

Dutch colonialists in the 1740's had chosen Simonstown, or Simon Stad as they called it, as a harbour for their trading ships and for the ships which would protect their trade routes. They chose it because the harbour entrance faces north and the Cape peninsular mountains would provide shelter from the north westerly winter winds.

Prior to the handover of the base to South Africa in 1955, the 'Simonstown Agreement' was signed. This would allow use of the base and its facilities to the Royal Navy for twenty years, expiring June 1975. As a youngster back in 1957 the Agreement seemed to me like it was forever. Now that I'm a village elder, pausing, resting on my spade from planting my first earlies – Pentland Javelins this year – going for flavour over bulk… and with the benefit of hindsight, were it up to me I would have held out for at least another seven years on the Agreement then our ships could have used the base during the Falklands war. In 1982 those that signed the Agreement on behalf of the UK back in the fifties, probably wished the same, as they leaned on their spades, having planted for flavour over bulk, or bulk over flavour – who cares.

Our first sight of the country was the lights of Port Elizabeth twinkling on the hillsides as we closed with land. We were eleven days out of Trincomalee. The next evening we would round Africa's southernmost point, Cape Agulhas, before preparing to enter harbour at Simonstown, part of False Bay, twenty miles to the south of Cape Town.

It was another of my boyhood heroes, Vasco de Gama, the Portuguese navigator who, sailing in the opposite direction to us, had rounded the Cape of Good Hope as he discovered the sea route to India.

Initially to us boy seamen the Cape of Good Hope seemed a beacon of modern civilization not unlike Europe, until we heard about apartheid, or apartness. Supposedly racial segregation but actually racial discrimination of the worst type, not unlike the Nazi tyranny our fathers had fought against. We were given a talk about this situation before our arrival and warned to steer clear of any involvement and not to break the racist laws, however distasteful we found them to be.

The animal kingdom, being above our human behaviour, was happy to share their waters with us. We watched southern right whales as they snorted and frolicked just offshore. Most of them had already migrated south after having calved. The whales were quite large being around fifteen metres in length. They fed as they swam, filtering plankton and tiny crustaceans from the water they constantly ingested. We watched as penguins clambered up the rocks and the otters hunting for fish. It should be a beautiful place, full of hope.

The journey into Cape Town was a train ride, a small train electric powered. The station had seats marked 'segs blanc', whites only. We chose to stand. The carriages were also segregated but we had no option. I can still remember the names of some of the many stops on the way in, Fish Hoek, Wine Hoek, Muizenburg and Ronderbosh. Sometimes we would choose to get off at one of these Towns. Here in our tropical whites we would be the centre of attention, a magnet for the local girls.

I remember the picturesque seaside town of Muizenburgh with its long sandy beaches, dancing under the stars on the pier, rocking and rolling to the new phenomenon, Elvis Presley, to Bill Haley whose 'Rock Around the Clock' started it all and to Carl Perkins 'Blue Suede Shoes', but Elvis was King!

Cape Town itself was nice. The view from atop the Table Top magnificent, mountains, rolling hills and vineyards. The notice board outside the Commander's office was filled with invitations from families wishing to extend hospitality to one or two of the crew, at their home, farm or vineyard. There were so many invitations that some of the duty watch were detailed off to go. In those days I was too self conscious to go and anyway us youngsters preferred the clubs, pubs and girls of Cape Town and Muizenburgh.

When it was time to sail for home, many budding romances had to be nipped in the bud. Tearful farewells on the jetty as the Royal Marine Band struck up 'wish me luck as you wave me goodbye'. We sailed minus a few of the crew who had fallen foul of the race laws, they would serve a harsh sentence before being allowed to return home.

I had never heard of the African National Congress at that time, nor of the young lawyers Nelson Mandela or Oliver Tambo. They had been accused of treason and of trying to overthrow the Government. Mandela was imprisoned in 1962 for 5 years, then, after escaping, he was again jailed spending 27 years, mostly at the infamous Robben Island, before being released in 1990. I'm pleased that the UK played a big part in the anti-apartheid campaign and efforts to release him. In 1994 Nelson Mandela became President of a National Unity Government and was awarded the Nobel Prize for Peace. His Truth and Reconciliation Commission helped to deal with the violence and human rights abuses by all sides of society.

A brief encounter

Leaving Simonstown, the Cape of Good Hope and the lights of Cape Town astern, we were 6,000 miles from home waters. Home for Superb had always been Chatham dockyard, built on the Medway estuary by Henry VIII and Elizabeth I to protect the approaches to London.

Although we could steam 8,000 miles at 16 knots we called in at Dakar, Senegal on the Cape Verde peninsula, to take on fuel. Economy wasn't the main consideration. We could open the throttles and be at 30 knots which would bring our range down to 2,000 miles. The main consideration was the projection of power, if needed. 'Homeward bound' may not mean the shortest route between two points. Better to have full tanks than to be forced to rendezvous with a Royal Fleet Auxiliary tanker to replenish at sea.

As far as I can remember, we arrived late evening at the fuelling jetty. There was no leave granted and we were back underway at daybreak. Perhaps this was meant to be a clandestine visit as for some reason we were maintaining radio and W.T. silence. I only know this because my elder brother, Ken, was on the bridge of the S.S. Roslin Castle, a Union Castle ship bound for the Cape of Good Hope and beyond. She was inbound to Dakar, to the fuelling jetties we had just departed. Ken recognized the Superb, having been aboard her, like myself, during 'Navy

Days' but also he knew we had been at Cape Town and were on our way to the U.K. He went to Roslin Castle's wireless office to try and pass a message to me but was told that they had been trying to get Superb to acknowledge their signals without any response.

I think Ken resented this snub by the senior service, as no longer does he dip his red ensign to me whenever I pass by.

Home Sweet home and a brat to catch a Mackeral

Our mid-terraced council house was supposedly a three bedroom, but really two bedrooms and a box room which became mum and dad's bedroom due to the ever increasing number of children. The front bedroom was for us four boys – three in one bed top to tail and one in the single bed. A couple of blankets topped off with old coats during the winter months, it was then that we would get an ice film on the insides of the metal framed windows – happy days!

Ken, the eldest boy, left at the age of 16 to train at the Merchant Navy Sea Training School, The Prince of Wales, in Norfolk. He was there during the east coat floods in 1951 which also created loss of life at nearby Canvey Island when the sea wall was breached and even closer to us at Tilbury which we overlooked from our hilltop position at Chadwell-St-Mary. While Ken and his fellow trainees were filling sand bags to repair sea walls at Sea Palling, us younger brothers were cadging lifts on the U.S. military trucks to trundle through the flood water at Tilbury. They had been called to evacuate those that needed to leave their homes and to help supply those that didn't. An army searchlight unit had set up shop on Chadwell Hill, opposite the church and just below the house where Daniel Defoe, the author, had stayed, or so the plaque says. He did also once live down in Tilbury where the searchlights would illuminate, bouncing their beams off the clouds, to assist the authorities who would be pumping out and restoring essential services once flood waters subsided and also probably to deter looters, burglars and other riff raff who wish to take advantage of others misfortunes.

Anyway that was all in the past, although still recent memories for those who had lost loved ones, by the time I arrived back home from the East Indies. Dad had come down to Chatham to meet the ship bringing Dave, my youngest brother, with him. They came aboard along with a throng of other relatives of the crew – must have been a thousand or so. I took Dad and Dave down to my messdeck to show them where and how I lived – it probably put Dave off as later in life he joined the army to become a bandsman and to study music. He must have had a talent for it as he now teaches at the Cologne School of Music.

A week or so later, the old home town looked the same as I stepped down from the train, except we had no railway line through Chadwell so I had probably taken a taxi ride from the Gravesend/Tilbury ferry, after having ridden the train from Chatham.

The most important person at home of course was our dear mum and I can't call to mind seeing her for the first time after all that time away. I only hope I made plenty of fuss of her, but knowing myself to be a bit thoughtless as a youngster I don't suppose I did.

My brother John was away at sea as was Ken whose ship had passed mine on her outbound journey. By persistent badgering John had got a deck boy's job on the Orient Liner 'Orion' despite having a perforated eardrum. He was now Australia bound. One of my closest friends from school days had joined the Navy about the same time I did. He was sent to HMS Ganges to train, after which he joined the destroyer HMS Corruna. I know that because he had sent my mum a Christmas card. I never have set eyes on him since – he's probably a retired Admiral now!

During the daytime youngsters would meet up in a café down the Old High Street to listen to the blaring juke-box music. In the evenings I would often meet up with lads home on leave from the merchant Navy at the 'Theobalds Arms' in Grays, a favourite with seamen. They would tell me their stories and adventures, most of which seemed a bit humdrum on ships that steered a straight course from point 'A' to point 'B', but I didn't say so. I didn't drink coffee or coca-cola only milk or beer, I must have averaged 3 pints of milk during the day and 4 pints of beer per evening during that leave. Apart from the pub I would go to the dancehall at Gravesend or to one of the cinemas at Grays. The Ritz and Regal are now long gone. The State cinema, now closed, is a grade 2 listed building. Built in 1938 in an art deco style it could seat a 2,200 audience. It has an illuminated Compton organ which rises up by lift from the orchestra pit. I can remember queuing at all three cinemas which is testament to their popularity during those days.

Grays itself took its name from the Norman Knight Anchetil (Henry) de Greye who was given the manor by Richard I in 1196. I don't suppose he could have been a most favoured knight or he would have got somewhere in Surrey. Anyways it was what lay under the ground that counted to the Victorians. They mined and exported the chalk around the globe by sea from the docks at Purfleet. The modern housing estate at Chafford Hundred is on Victorian landfill which covers one of the chalk pits. The Lion gorge and the Warren gorge are also evidence of the chalk mining. The huge Lakeside shopping complex is built inside the chalk workings from that period.

My younger brother Mick has only memories of me pressing my uniforms getting them ready for my return to the ship, whereas my kid sister, Kassy, about seven at the time, says that I used her as bait to attract the older girls, she being cute, pigtailed and doll-like. Like a brat to catch a mackerel I said. I don't know if any took the bait as Kassy is still alive and kicking, well alive and typing anyway. She tells me now, fifty plus years too late, that I was in demand by the girls, but I think at the time I was oblivious to the fact.

I soon tired being on leave with nothing substantial to do and was not sorry to head back to Chatham and to the ship which was readying to sail.

A day trip down The Clyde

I had spent two or three months at HMS Harrier on the Pembrokeshire coast to qualify as a radar plotter. I trained on surface ships navigation, gunnery and air warning radars which I was destined never to use. I also trained to direct fighter aircraft, speaking directly to the pilots and had to learn all of the jargon to do so.

My next posting was to HMS Adamant, depot ship to the 3rd submarine squadron, at its base in the Gareloch which is a spur off of the river Clyde. I have heard people, who know no better, laugh that she rarely goes to sea. That is because they are ignorant of the importance of these valuable and complex ships. They need to be in a secure, well protected anchorage, but be able to change location should the operational circumstance dictate.

Aboard these ships are torpedo, periscope and engineering workshops. Up to a dozen submarines are her brood, which she has to maintain and keep supplied which fresh and frozen provisions, as well as clothing, charts, ropes and wires. She also supplies fresh water and fuel via her tenders. A floating dock is also available. When submarines are alongside their crews generally live aboard the depot ship and are fed in her dining halls. Operations and planning staff officers aboard the depot ship direct the missions that the squadron's boats will undertake.

My small part in all of this was to work aboard the diving tender Yo-yo. Propellers of submarines had to be checked before embarking on a patrol, any small inclusion on the blades surface could create cavitation, the noise of which would make the boat an easy to track target. Usually I tended the lines of the specialist divers when they carried out more difficult tasks.

I soon began to realise that the crews of the submarines had a different outlook to the rest of us. Although they seemed to shamble about and have very little outward respect for uniform or rank, they also appeared to be very professional.

Aboard Adamant I was told "Don't go down there it's a submariners mess" I also noticed that Adamant's duty officer, doing evening rounds, didn't go down there either. When ashore one night in Helensburgh I was told "Don't go in there it's a submariners bar".

Later I realised it wasn't that they were unfriendly or belligerent it was because they were a close knit community, having common bonds they understood and respected each others pressures, failings and eccentricities. Through my work I made acquaintance with a few submariners and was invited aboard their submarines on a couple of occasions at 'up spirits', for gulpers, half a tot, or whatever although being officially under age. The other mess members would be polite and friendly but I didn't feel I could be one of them unless I became one of them by qualifying.

In those days submariners were volunteers. With this in mind I requested through my divisional officer to join the submarine service. He made arrangements for me to have a day trip on one of the squadron's boats which had been in the floating dock having some repairs and was now going out to check the result. I think it was a 'T' class but I can't remember for sure.

I was on her bridge at harbour stations and stood listening to reports as various equipment was tested and noticed the forward hydroplanes turn out, were tilted forward, then tilted backwards, then they were turned back in. I watched as the deck crew took in and stowed the lines and wire ropes below the casing. They then lowered the bollards level with the casing before disappearing down the hatch into the hull of the submarine. The casing officer reported "Casing secured" to the captain before he too went below.

It was explained to me that all maneuvering in harbour was done using main motors (electric power). They had almost instant response – also they could go astern whereas the main diesel engines could not. Once the submarine reached clear water the main engines coughed into life and I could see the muffled exhausts protruding from the after casing, the water spray from the mufflers dampening down the exhaust smoke.

I was sent below as we proceeded down the Clyde to accompany the first lieutenant and outside E.R.A. as they checked the submarine was properly opened up for diving. I followed them as they worked their way from the forward tube space to the after ends checking everything, valves, vents, hatches, gauges. It just seemed a maze to me. The first lieutenant, usually known as the 'Jimmy' by the crew or 'No. 1' by the captain, once satisfied reported to the captain "Boat opened up for diving sir". I was surprised to notice the captain was also only a lieutenant. He replied "Thank you No. 1, go to patrol routine". These actions had turned us from what was essentially a surface ship to a submarine, able to dive in an instant.

I stood in the control room, tucked out of the way, watching as the helmsman responded to orders passed via the voice pipe from the bridge above. The captain was taking bearings through the periscope with the signalman reading off the bearings from the scale above the captain's head, passing them to the navigator to fix our position on the chart. The captain checked the chart and the depth in fathoms beneath our keel, went back to the periscope, took a quick all round sweep, snapped the periscope handles up and as the periscope slid down into its well, ordered the officer of the watch to come below and dive the submarine on the klaxon.

First the lookout came down the tower ladder and stood at the bottom looking up as the officer of the watch followed him through the upper hatch pressing the klaxon twice as he did so. He slammed the hatch shut, the lookout peering up reported "One clip on", then "Both clips on" and moved aside as the O.O.W. came down into the control room. I was startled by the rasping noise of the klaxon blasts but even more so by the activity this caused. It seemed as though I was on a film set, how Alice must have felt when she fell down the rabbit hole into a strange world. Crew members pushed past me, some changing positions with those who had been on watch. Two others manned the fore and aft planes. I was aware that the main engines had stopped, the main vents had been opened to flood ballast tanks, the forward hydroplanes had been turned out and now the planesmen were responding to the Jimmy's orders (he carrying out the C.O.'s instruction "Down to 60ft and back to periscope depth five degrees of bubble"). I was aware of telegraph orders to the main motors, of the lower lid being shut, once they checked the upper lid was sealed, to isolate the tower from the main pressure hull. They left the ladder rigged as we were not going to be dived for a long period. As we leveled off and returned to 45ft the captain motioned with a flick of his hand and the periscope slid up, he flicked down the handles and rose from his crouching position, eyes glued to the scope as he swiveled around. As he moved his eyes away to speak to the Jimmy I could see sunlight reflected in his eyes. The Jimmy was flicking light indicator switches which passed orders to the ballast pump operator for him to pump, or flood, water into or out of tanks to enable the Jimmy to catch a trim. He wouldn't be satisfied until the boat could be kept level and at the desired depth using the hydroplanes, while the motors were at slow speed.

The skipper was obviously satisfied with the trim and the watertight integrity as he said "Very good No. 1, shut main vents, take her down to 120ft". Shortly after this the tannoy announced "Red watch, watch diving", the crowd in the control room thinned out and I thinned out with them to the forward mess. Even with my ignorance of most that was going on around me, I could see that this was an experienced, well trained and self assured crew, carrying out what to them were routine actions.

As we surfaced and headed back up the Clyde toward the Gareloch I was determined to go ahead with my request. A couple of days later I was summoned to the office of Captain S/M3, Captain Ian McGeoch (later Admiral Sir Ian McGeoch KCB, DSO, DSC, Flag Officer Submarines). He fixed his one good eye on me, the other had been injured during one of his heroic actions during WWII and asked me why I wanted to become a submariner. I said "I want to become a man like you sir" which made him chuckle. He shook my hand and wished me well. My service documents were stamped and noted 'recommended for service in submarines' and signed 'I McGeoch'.

PART 3

Submarine Service
The Cold War Years

Submarine training and S.E.T.T

It was late summer when I reported to the main gate at HMS Dolphin, Fort Blockhouse, Gosport, where I would join up with others from who knows where, to form a class for basic submarine training. I was directed by the Quartermaster to what was known as Dolphin II. Arriving there I could see that it was a collection of wartime vintage brick huts, a separate compound within high steel-mesh fencing. Here I met up with others; a collection of odd-bods also recently arrived. Glancing at the specialisation badges on their right arms I noticed a couple of U.W's (underwater weapons), a sparker (wireless operator), who it turned out was a cheerful Maltese and a tall thin gunlayer. During the course of the afternoon others began to drift in, amongst them a Chef who looked as if he had just stepped out of a boxing ring having lost the bout, a couple of sonar operators and a radio electrical mechanic who later would serve with me in the Mediterranean, servicing the radar and intelligence equipment that I operated.

I think there were about fifteen of us, all quite young, 18-20 years of age. A couple were still ordinary seamen which I would have been without the three months accelerated advancement to able seaman, granted to me by Captain McGeoch on my annual assessment. Some of these lads had never even seen a submarine, at least I had served at the service's busiest operational base, drunk rum with a few submariners, seen them at work and had taken a day trip and a dip below the surface, although I had little idea of what made a submarine tick.

We drew our bedding from the store and were sorting out our bunks and putting kit into our lockers when in strolled a tall Chief Petty Officer Coxswain. He asked us to gather round. After introducing himself he took a quick roll-call which included our nicknames, as a means of introduction to each other. He gave us a brief outline, the form the course would take, this included for me and the other R.P.3's (radar plot, 3rd class) the fact that we would do a short conversion to submarine radar and plots here at Dolphin II. Most of the others would do their conversion courses elsewhere in the base.

The course he said would start in the morning which I think was Wednesday. On Monday we would spend two days at the submarine escape tank (about three hundred yards from where we now stood). He told us that every submariner from the Flag Officer (a Vice Admiral) down to the lowest of the low (us) had to qualify and then every couple of years take a refresher course. "You will enjoy the experience", he said. For our part we looked a bit doubtful. "Remember that you are all volunteers, if you don't want to be here you might as well go now", he said. "What you get up to in the evenings is up to you as long as you are bright eyed and bushy tailed come 0830 each day. I won't tell you to do anything twice, but don't be afraid to ask questions, our classroom is in the hut next door. Here endeth the first lesson." With that he turned on his heels and disappeared from whence he had come.

The course would last about two months in total but at its end we would not be qualified to wear the submarine badge, which in those days we called a 'sausage on a stick', worn on the left cuff, but later changed to the 'dolphins' as worn today on the left breast. Continuation training, known as Part Three, would commence once part of a submarine's crew and would take up to three months, at the end of which one would need to convince the boat's First Lieutenant that you had a good knowledge of the boat and its systems.

I liked the informality and humour of the Coxswain. We would do some straight line drawings of the various systems, he would show us on the chalkboard different valves and their functions then we would walk as a gaggle down to one of the boats at the jetty, where he would take us through the system so we could see it in the flesh, amongst the tangle of pipes and cables. Wherever we went everyone seemed to know the Coxswain calling him by his nickname (which I can't remember) from officers down to bilge rats.

We all worked hard and would quiz each other before going ashore in the evenings, none of us wanted to be returned to gens (as we called the general service Navy). On the Friday we went through the basic principles of the free ascent escape and what we called the BIBS, the built in breathing system, a source of unpolluted air to breathe during the flooding up of the escape compartment and while waiting one's turn to ascend to the surface. The atmosphere within a sunken submarine may lack oxygen and contain hydrogen and chlorine if seawater mixed with the battery acid. The BIBS high pressure air bottle groups are fixed to the outside of the pressure hull, one forrard above the torpedo stowage compartment, which is used as an escape compartment and one aft above the engine room, also an escape compartment. In both cases the casing is strengthened with wooden planking to help protect them.

Inside the respective areas of the hull we were shown the various valves and the reducers which brought the H.P. air down to a breathable level, 100lbs per sq.inch above the compartment pressure. During later training in the tank we would be taught how to expel this extra pressure from our lungs as we rose toward the surface with sea pressure lessening throughout the upward journey, as escaping with burst lungs would bring no joy.

Whatever boat I subsequently served aboard, by choice I slept in the torpedo stowage compartment which of course was the forrard escape compartment, usually I opted for the top bunk where inches from my face would be one of the quick release sockets into which the male adaptor of a breathing tube would be plugged. The sockets were about twelve inches apart in a ring main around the compartment, enough for the whole crew, plus any extra personnel, to breathe clean air during the escape procedure. Fluorescent marked metal cabinets around the upper parts of the compartment contained the lifejackets, immersion suits, the breathing tubes and other necessary items such as nose clips and emergency torches.

I chose not to remind myself that all this was well and dandy as long as we happened to be in waters shallow enough for the submarine to reach the bottom in one piece, to be able to flood up the compartment and make our escape. Most of our time we would be operating out in open oceans so deep that the pressure hull, in a negative buoyancy state, would implode long before reaching the seabed.

It was not without trepidation that we looked forward to Monday morning and the tank, the thought of it the only shackle on an otherwise free weekend.

The long arm of coincidence, that has played a role in my life on a number of occasions, recently brought me into contact with he who was the scratcher (2nd Coxswain) on my first submarine the 'Tudor'. It turns out that his wife is a longtime friend of one of my wife's closest friends. Anyway we met up again about fifty years since we first served together, him as a Petty Officer me, initially, as an Able Seaman Part Three Trainee. He had also trained at St Vincent and like me was in Anson Division. He had joined 'Tudor' after spending two years at the SETT as a swim boy. The following account details Mike's experiences at the tank:

When I joined the submarine service in the mid 1950's I was trained in escape procedure using both the Davis escape apparatus and the recently adopted free ascent method. The Davis breathing set was complicated and involved breathing oxygen which was unsafe below 32ft. Our main training took place in the newly commissioned 100ft tank which is still in use today, using free ascent.

It was after having served over two years on submarines that I applied for a posting to the tank. This was a sought after two year posting and I was surprised to be quickly accepted. The staff of the tank were commanded by an experienced submarine C.O., A First Lieutenant assisted him. A Senior Coxswain known as the Chief of the Tank and six other Coxswains were instructors. Manning the 60ft and 30ft chambers and assisting trainees in the tank were 'swim boys' – drawn from Stoker petty officers and 2nd Coxswains like me. The medical staff were a Surgeon Lieutenant and a Petty Officer Sick Berth Attendant. The escape equipment was maintained by a civilian expert who was the fount of many a salty yarn. The civilian cleaner, reputedly over 70, had ten floors to clean so had to be assisted in this by us swim boys.

The tank had to be available and ready to assist in any submarine emergency so was continually manned. As usual single men were used when possible at weekends and bank holidays, which seemed to prompt a number of weddings amongst the staff.

We would hold an open day each year for our families and friends when we would entertain them with a few tricks of the trade. Four of us would descend to the bottom in a diving bell, place buckets over our heads and rise to the surface using only the air trapped within the bucket. Some of the instructors would take a lungful of air, drop to the bottom of the tank, then climb back to the surface using ropes fixed to the tankside. Lung capacity varies person to person, that of the tank staff varied between 5 and 7.5 litres, during the time served in the tank this capacity increased by at least half a litre for most of us.

The training classes would arrive on a Monday and be given lectures and demonstrations of the equipment and its use. This included the life jacket which each escapee would wear. This was fitted with a relief valve to vent off the pressure inside it as the wearer rose to the surface. As with human lungs a burst life jacket would be useless to assist the wearer to float on reaching the surface. The immersion suit of double skinned rubberized material was also demonstrated, only a few of the escapees would actually wear one. It was designed to be inflated once on the surface to assist in floatation but also keep the wearer insulated from the cold. An absorbent padded nappy would be worn inside the suit to prevent body fluids from pooling around the lower back and chilling the kidneys and other organs which could be fatal if rescue ships were slow to arrive. If these suits had been available at the time of the sinking of the 'Truculant' many lives could have been saved. To end this first session a short film describing what it might be like to escape from a sunken submarine was shown.

Later in the morning small groups of the class were sat in a recompression chamber and 'taken down' to the equivalent of 200ft by the introduction of H.P. air. This put the trainees under a certain amount of stress as it was noisy, the atmosphere became cloudy and hot, eardrums would pop and the trainees would learn to equalise the pressure in their ears. Voices would become high pitched and comical – sounding like Mickey Mouse. The instructors would be watching each individual to weed out any that couldn't handle the stress.

Those suitable were taken to the top of the tank not just to let them look down into it but to check each individual for buoyancy. This is dependent on the ratio of fat to bone, usually a well-covered person is very buoyant and the slim person not so. Another factor of course is the individual's lung capacity. Most sink to just below the surface then bob up. Those that tended to sink like a stone when they let go the side, we would keep an extra eye on.

During the final session on the first day, groups of trainees were taken into the 30ft chamber which had an entry into the tank. The chamber was flooded to allow the pressure to equalize so the entry door to the tank could be opened. One at a time the trainees left the chamber, were steadied and checked by the swimboys, to ensure that the arms were by the side, the feet together, that the trainee was expelling breath and only then allowed to proceed to the surface by the buoyancy of the lifejacket. This same procedure was carried out again but this time from the 60ft chamber.

The next day, day two, the trainees would do the 100ft escape from the chamber below the tank. This was laid out to resemble the inside of a submarine with the built in breathing system. The escape hatch had the twill trunk around it which would be secured at deck level. This prevented air in the compartment escaping while pressure was equalizing to allow the escape hatch to be opened. The escapees could have their heads above the water's surface while breathing clean air through their breathing tubes. One at a time they would have to duck down and enter the twill trunk to make good their escape. As before they would be checked by the swimboys before allowing them to ascend.

On arriving at the surface and having left the water the trainees would stand for four minutes which was time enough for staff to be sure that no air had passed into the blood stream through the lung walls. If it had, an air embolism would form within that four minutes and would lodge in the brain causing the person to collapse. On the rare occasion this occurred (only twice during my two years service in the tank) the sufferer would be taken 'down' to the equivalent of 200ft in the recompression chamber until the now compressed embolism dispersed naturally, this could take up to two days. The nearest member of staff would go into the recompression chamber with him and stay for the two days without any relief. Compensation of 4d (old money) per minute would be paid to that staff member which could perhaps earn him up to £48. A nice bonus in the days when annual salary was less than £1,500.

I can't pretend that I enjoyed being under pressure in the chamber even though it wasn't a new experience for me as it was part of my shallow water diving course. I knew how to clear my ears and found the noise no problem, what I disliked was the heat, but that is wherever, not just in a recompression chamber. Two members of our class had problems, one I think suffered a perforated eardrum the other was stress related. When we got back to the hut in the evening their beds were stripped, lockers empty and they were gone. We were now thirteen in number – lucky for some!

Looking down from the top of the tank to the bottom 100ft below, the water clear, well lit all the way down, was not inviting. It was like staring into the abyss, a journey I had to take to be that what I wanted to be. As I looked down a swim boy emerged from the 60ft pod at the side of the tank. Expecting him to rise to the surface I was amazed to see him descend to the bottom. He casually checked something there for what seemed an age before slowly ascending – a stream of bubbles beating him to the surface, his hands and arms were tight to his sides and his head was slightly tilted back. As he neared the surface I could see the goggles he wore to protect his eyes. On his nose was a spring clip – he looked for all the world a frog of a man, not a frogman as he had no flippers.

Once I had completed the 30ft ascent I was quite happy to do the 60ft as well, not much different to shallow water diving, the lifejacket made for a quick ascent. En route upwards from 60ft I was aware of a swim-boy checking my progress to straighten me up, they told me afterwards that like a few others I headed toward the far side of the tank instead of straight upwards.

I think for most of us day two made us question why we had volunteered for this, but we all tried to appear nonchalant. We filed into the 100ft chamber and were sorting out and plugging in our breathing tubes having donned and inflated our lifejackets. Standing between Grumpy the Chef and me, was a tall lean Sub-Lieutenant, one of a group of four, also doing their basic training. He looked at me and in his cut-glass public school accent he said "Bloody hell, they're going to flood this place with water soon". "Would you prefer champagne sir?", sez I. It was the only time I heard old Grumpy laugh. Thereafter we knew the subbie as Champagne Charlie. The name followed him throughout his service despite the fact that his parents had named him Lancelot or Rupert or something. Little did Grumpy know then, that he would be feeding Champagne Charlie with his version of pot mess and other of his culinary treats for the next year or so on the 'S' class boat they both joined after training.

Grumpy was cooking at the 'last chance saloon'. General service had convinced him to join submarines by saying that was the only chance of him ever getting his hook (leading rate). In other words their loss was also our loss.

Anyway, breathing out all the way we made it up to the surface. The tension all gone, we were like excited school kids on our way back to Dolphin II saying how much we enjoyed it all, quickly forgetting how keyed up we'd been.

On completing training some were immediately posted, joining boats as far afield as Australia or Canada. With a couple of the others I went into spare crew in Dolphin, eagerly awaiting joining one of the new Porpoise class or whatever. When my posting finally came through it was to one of the oldest boats in the service, having its final re-fit in Scotland!

A rose by any other name

The boys gave me a good send off as back to Scotland I headed, this time not toward Glasgow and the Gareloch but towards Edinburgh and Rosyth dockyard. When eventually the night train reached the terminus I felt tired, cold and cramped after the uncomfortable ride in the packed and jolting carriage.

Edinburgh has two rail stations as I remember, one is called Waverley. Anyway I had to struggle from one to the other with my large heavy kitbag and suitcase to catch an onward train, cross the Forth Bridge and reach Dunfermline. There I would be met and taken to the old air station at Donibristle, where the crew were living while the submarine was completing its refit in Rosyth dockyard.

We lived in a large brick built barrack room in the centre of which was a cast iron stove with a cast iron chimney pipe which led vertically up and through the roof. If we kept the stove continually stoked up it threw out enough heat to warm the bunks within ten feet of it. Those on the periphery might as well be in the middle of a field. Being one of the last to join and also amongst the junior of the juniors, I was on the outer edge of the periphery – in fact closest to the door which, every time it was opened, sent any icy blast around my bed space.

'Deaks' the killik torpedoman would organize a scavenging party whenever our coal stock got low, to raid the wardrooms stock or anyone else's stock that wasn't under lock and key.

Unpacking my kitbag into my metal locker I discovered one reason it had been so heavy – the lads from spare crew had put a concrete block, wrapped in my overalls, half way down as a memento.

The next day I joined the rest of the lads on the pussers bus to where the boat rested in dry dock – well the hull was, but the casing had been removed in large sections which were scattered along the jetty. For the next few days I was using a windy hammer (as we called the pneumatic paint chippers) to bring the steel casing to bare metal ready for priming and repainting with a thick brown undercoat, topped with a shiny black topcoat. Like Henry Ford the first sea lord said you can have your submarines any colour you like as long as they are black. Apart from our NATO number S126 painted in white about 2ft 6ins high and the shiny brass handrail around the bridge structure, we were totally black – end of story.

Looking at the casing and at the machinery being returned from workshops and from the manufacturers I remember hoping that someone somewhere had the handbook for this old underwonder boat which I would soon be living on. The only reassuring thing, none of the experienced submariners seemed at all concerned. The only thing leading torpedoman Deaks seemed concerned with was 'liberating' any non-standard, or customised things, that he could find on board the reserve fleet ships that were parked around the dockyard. He would take me and any other willing idiot he could find, we'd wear overalls and plimsols. We mainly kept watch at strategic points, namely the top of the ship's gangway and ladders going down or up to where Deaks was rummaging. We would look out for dockyard police or reserve fleet officers or P.O.'s who would check the moorings and bilges of these ships at intervals. Deaks' view was that he was only transferring items from one Navy ship to another. He would have made a good Special Forces commando as he loved explosives, detonators and timers, luckily he never blew up any of our warships.

Another 'liberation' that happened at this time was when the French Navy handed back one of our old submarines (I think it was an 'S' boat) and we had to check her out inside. Our chief stoker found that one of her fresh water tanks was half full of red wine. As it was tested and found to be good, we didn't waste it. These sorts of things weren't worth bothering our officers with, as they would be concerned with 'proper channels' and filling out a 'found wine' form or something!

When I was informed that I had been posted to join my first boat and that its name was 'Tudor' I wasn't really surprised as coincidence has played a part in my life many times. I was in Tudor house at my secondary school at Grays, Essex. For my history exams at that school I had written of the life of Henry Tudor who came from the house of Richmond. It was he who defeated Richard III in battle to end the War of the Roses.

The union rose, the floral emblem of England is the Tudor rose, which is an amalgamation of the red rose of the house of Lancaster and the white rose of the house of York. The rose is often shown divided in different ways. That on our submarine crest is shown divided vertically red to the left, white to the right. When I met the girl, who later in life would become my wife, she told me that her grammar school in Reading had the Tudor rose as their crest and that her family came from Richmond. The house we live in now we named 'Richmond', the architect who drew the plans for its conversion from a bungalow to a house, drew Tudor roses within its exterior screeded panels. When I asked him why, he said we could have any number of different emblems and the rose was just a suggestion. Needless to say we had exactly what he suggested.

I've often wondered how a submarine crew is assembled – do 'they', the mysterious drafting office staff, look closely at the individual and try to put a squarish peg into a square hole or do they just say "Ah, we need one of that rank or specialization and two of those, plus a T.I, a chief stoker, etc, etc." However it was done, the crew converges from all points of the compass, some from overseas bases or submarines, some straight from promotion courses, some from spare crew posts at home or abroad and in our case a high proportion of the junior rates came from basic submarine training course, I was one of those. We were known as 'Part 3 Trainees', not yet fully fledged submariners entitled to wear the submarine badge, until we had completed and passed this Part 3. We would need to satisfy the First Lieutenant after two or three months, that we knew the boat and its systems and of our ability to operate much of its equipment. We had to untangle the maze of pipes and valves and relate them to the straight line drawings of our training course. Joining a boat in refit was a help once the tangle of the dockyard workmen's air hoses, electrical cables and other equipment was removed and we could see the wood through the trees. The various supply lines, distilled water, fresh water, sea water, circulating water, high pressure air, low pressure air, hydraulic to 1,500 lbs per sq. inch, oleo fluid for external hydraulic power, lubricating oil, fuel oil, the main line and trim line. All of these and others we had to paint with their identification markings, a combination of coloured rings close to their operating valves.

One of the last jobs I noticed being done by a dockyard craftsman was the french polishing of internal woodwork. It seemed slightly incongruous to me, watching this dedicated man painstakingly working amongst the chaos to achieve a high quality finish. We must have been amongst the last submarines to have polished woodwork, like the library of a stately home, warm and cosy. Conversion and new builds would be finished in Formica, light, bright and garish. You would almost think you were in a supermarket, rather than the grocers.

Gradually the jig-saw was coming together and it was time to test for missing pieces. We would be carrying out our own vacuum test, before taking the boat out for test dives to check the water tightness of pressure hull fittings. We would shut the hatches and by running the blower, pump air into the main ballast tanks from inside the boat to create a slight vacuum, before checking for air leaking into the boat. The barometer would tell us of any drop in this vacuum.

The Tudor was an early build of the Group 2 'T' class, with riveted hull, so not suitable for conversion. Other boats of this class were streamlined, one of which was the Talent the last boat I served on, another was the Tireless, which I have mentioned in a later chapter. The Tudor it seemed was not thought suitable for streamlining probably for the same reason as the Aurochs, the only 'A' class boat that I served on, i.e. poor condition.

Initially on Tudor we would operate down to 300ft. I think the Captain took her down to 350ft on our test dives. Later during the commission we were limited to 250ft because of the poor condition of the hull, not always a reassuring thought, but we consoled ourselves that their lordships had probably calculated a safety margin on top of this.

The Tudor now looked very much a purposeful submarine having eleven 21" torpedo tubes, six internal at the bow, above them under the casing were two external tubes. Abaft the bridge, again under the casing, were two more external tubes, firing aft, angled outward to clear the after planes and the stern. The final tube, also external, was right aft under the casing. Obviously once these externals had been fired it wouldn't be possible to reload them until we returned to harbour. As you can see, these boats as built packed a huge punch, however the drag created through the water by the casing needed to envelope these extra projections meant a penalty on underwater speed and the ability to run silent. Speed was now of the essence, to be able to deliver a snap attack and make a speedy withdrawal from the scene afterwards. Counter attack by fast surface escorts using modern anti-submarine weapons was deadly and probably fatal for any that loitered.

We would make an ideal target for our own anti-submarine warships and helicopters to hone the training of their attack teams. Towards this end, once the boat and the crew were deemed competent by completing a hectic 'work up' period and inspection, we would be based at the home of anti-submarine warfare training at Portland, Dorset.

A Trip around the Isles, a bit of a flummox and a word in a pigs ear

As the crow flies, give or take a few flaps of the wing, it is about fifty miles from Rosyth dockyard in Edinburgh's backyard to Faslane home of the 3rd Submarine Squadron nestled in the protected and sheltered still water of the Gareloch on the outskirts of Glasgow. After completion of our test dives and various engine and machinery proving checks to the satisfaction of the Captain and Engineer Officer and whoever else accepted her on behalf of the Navy, it was time to put, not only the submarine, but the diverse bunch of us the crew through a rigorous month long ordeal known as the 'work up' to hone our teamwork and be ready to join the fleet.

We couldn't, however, travel as the crow does. Looking at the charts as I laid them out in order in the drawers below the control room's chart table I could see that the sea route entailed a tricky voyage of some 700 miles. Following the coast north past Aberdeen and crossing the Moray Firth between Fraserburgh and John O'Groats navigating between the coast and the Orkney Islands, before rounding Cape Wrath, through the Minch's between the Western Isles and the Isle of Skye, leaving Tiree and then Islay to port before rounding the Mull of Kintyre to pass between Sanda and the Ailsa Craig, passing Arran to enter the Clyde and to make our way up to the Gareloch.

Although I was the only one of my basic training class on board, others from previous classes had joined before me. In total I think about eighteen of us were part three trainees. We had a lot to learn and quickly, no room in a submarine's crew for passengers. Each had to play his part as a watch member. We would have to lean on the experienced, older A.B's, the killiks (leading rates) and the P.O's. Although I had qualified in general service radar this trip during a bleak Scottish winter through rocky narrows in poor visibility would be my first experience of radar watchkeeping and with only one R.P. per watch as they say you are on your own Jack, coupled with acting as the navigator's yeoman for the first time I was on a steep learning curve.

Passing Ailsa Craig was a reminder to me of my first dunk in a submarine, as the skipper of that boat had used the rock to fix his diving position, hard to believe that was some six months ago. On arrival at Faslane, in company with the others of the attack team, two days were spent at the attack teacher at Rothsay, Bute, practicing attacks on convoys and submarine targets. Back aboard the boat, time was spent at the torpedo firing ranges at Loch Long which, as its name implies, is a long loch. This was mainly for the benefit of the underwater weapons department but most of us seamen would be involved bringing aboard reload torpedoes. A spur off of Loch Long is Loch Goil, which is where we then headed to carry out sound trials. We would moor and dive between two buoys to sit on the bottom. The idea was to run motors and auxiliary pumps and various other machinery to enable boffins, using listening devices, coupled to their shoreside hut, to record the acoustic signature and pinpoint where further noise reduction measures were needed.

We spent time at sea to practice attacks and to carry out evolutions and emergency drills under the critical eye of Commander S/M. For instance he could perhaps order our Captain to change depth from 300ft to 150ft at full ahead group up, using 10 degrees of angle. Then, while this was being carried out, suddenly order full astern to meet the same depth. This meant the fore and after planesmen had to reverse roles, the after planesman now keeping the depth and the fore planesman maintaining the desired angle rather than the depth. This in itself could result in a few gyrations and a bit of a flummox, but just as normal control was resuming Commander S/M would order foreplanes in emergency control. The forendsman would work flat out to by-pass the ram and get into hand control, but however fast he worked, there was an inevitable delay. During this time with the Captain trying to maintain control, at the behest of Commander S/M, the ballast pump operator would report loss of suction, with the pump having to be re-primed. While all this was going on, a fire in the forward battery compartment was declared. A cool head was needed for the skipper to meet the original objective and just as he was close to doing so Commander S/M would move the goal posts, the goalie and perhaps some of the crew to a mysterious illness or noxious gas. To be a good Commander S/M it helped to be a sadist with nerves of steel, after all he was in the same boat as us while he seemed bent on its destruction, all we wanted was to return to our normal routine, to 'tot time' and the like – although at this stage being about nineteen years of age I was too young to be present at 'up spirits'.

Humour often carried us through. During the latter stage of our trip around the Isles, that which our Queen took most summer months aboard the Royal Yacht Britannia, as we passed the Isle of Skye the sun broke through and the day became pleasant and warm. Along with a few others I crammed up on the bridge to enjoy the views and the fresh air. Being in 'passage routine' we were not unlike a surface ship, not opened up for diving, the cotter pins were in the main vents to prevent any accidental flooding of main ballast tanks. For this reason available space was the only limitation the officer of the watch would put on a request through the helmsman's voicepipe for permission to come on the bridge. With us on the bridge were two members of an American University Ornithology Society studying the winter migration of the lesser striped duck billed chuff (or some other rare bird unknown to us herring gull watchers).

Now just aft of the cone shaped brass funnel of the voicepipe (which led down to the helmsman's position in the control room below) was another cone shaped funnel, although lower down, at convenient waist-high level. This is what we knew as the 'pigs ear' used as a urinal for the bridge crew to enable them to relieve themselves without the need for a relief to do so. The tube led down to allow the urine to discharge overboard to sea, keeping the bridge sweet. Deaks was up with me and was talking to the two university types. Suddenly pretending the pigs ear was the voicepipe he leant over close to it and twice called into it "Control room – bridge" and of course got no answer. He said to Professor Potts standing next to him "I'll wake the bugger up" he whipped out his john thomas and took a pee down his make believe voicepipe. The look on the face of that refined and learned American gentleman was a sight to behold and has remained with me over the years. I only hope he got a glimpse of his duck billed chuff.

Norwegian hospitality

Alongside the depot ship 'Adamant' were two trots of submarines. The after trot consisted of three boats – inboard alongside the depot ship, the visiting Norwegian 'Ula', a British built 'U' Class of wartime vintage. Alongside her was a 'T' conversion and we were the outboard boat.

Ula was ready for sea so the other two boats had to let her out. With just the Jimmy and the duty watch on board, the plan was for us to let go and move out astern, the 'T' conversion to 'open her legs' which meant she kept her head rope taut and then maneuvered so her stern swung out allowing Ula to follow us out astern.

It was a freezing cold winter's morning with a couple of inches of snow covering the hillsides that surround the Loch. We should have been wearing lifejackets but weren't. I was wearing working dress with submarine sweater over. On my feet I had thick socks with steaming boots. We let go the lines and pulled the gangplank inboard as we moved astern into the middle of the Loch. I jumped down onto the curved ballast tanks so I could push up on the plank to allow it to clear the deck ringbolts, whilst the others swung the plank inboard. As I pushed up, my boots slipped on the wet steel tanks, pitching me into the freezing water of the Loch.

The boat was moving fast astern and I was soon out of heaving line range. Most of the lads on the casing were laughing at first, but soon they realized it was serious. Luckily the quick thinking bunting tosser (signalman) on the bridge immediately threw the horseshoe lifebelt as far as he could in my direction. I had already kicked off my steaming boots but my thick clothing was fast becoming waterlogged. I struggled to swim as far as the lifebelt and I was already feeling the effect of the icy water.

The Norwegian captain aboard the Ula had seen my predicament and was already maneuvering Ula to within heaving line distance. I caught their line and the casing crew hauled me up on to their out-turned foreplanes and then onto the casing. I had been to Norway on more than one occasion. During a visit to Oslo some of us lived ashore at the Haraldsheim youth hostel – it was like seventh heaven as most of the other residents were female backpackers from the US and Canada and some Norwegians. I have met many Norwegians and liked them immensely although they seemed rather stolid and humourless. Once I rather shakily stood up the Ula's casing officer quite formally said "Welcome aboard". I could neither laugh nor thank him because my teeth were chattering like a flamenco dancer's castanets, but it did make me realize that under a dour exterior a sense of humour lurked. Once down in their Control Room I stripped off my sodden clothing and stood naked, shivering and shaking until someone handed me a towel. They produced some black woollen working dress for me to don and one of the Norwegian officers handed me a tumbler full of some spirit, probably brandy, which I downed in one. They had to return alongside Adamant to let me disembark. I never again worked on deck without a lifejacket.

A Seat in the Sand

On completion of our successful work-up we headed south, not to Gosport the base of our squadron, the 1st, but to Portland where together with our sister 'T' 'Thule' and two S boats, the 'Scorcher' and 'Seneschal' (I think) we would berth alongside 'Chaser' a tank landing craft which acted as our mother ship. She was hardly de luxe comfort, but we liked the whole set up. It was laid back Navy. We were tucked away from the grey funnel line, our name for the regular Navy. The biggest snag, in my book, was the road leading from the dockyard gate into Portland, where we'd catch the bus to Weymouth to the bright lights and holidaymakers (well the female ones we sought) led us right past the rats nest of regulating staff. They would try and find some dress code contravention to send us back to correct. I think they worked for the Russians as they certainly weren't on our side. The only place we knew we wouldn't bump into them was at sea, at the sharp end.

Chaser had a good shower/wash room, like a portacabin, on her upper deck, always had plenty of hot water as well as a drying room, which was handy as we couldn't carry much uniform clothing aboard. Another luxury to us was that her tank decks were laid out as bunk spaces which we could use when not duty watch on board.

Portland was the main anti-submarine training base for frigates of our

Navy and some other NATO navies, notably the Dutch and the Germans, as well as for the sonar-dipping Wessex helicopters based on Portland.

For their initial training we would act as a 'clockwork mouse' trundling up and down either at periscope depth or at 120ft (we never kept any depth in between the two as 120ft was the minimum to give clearance between us and the keels of the large ships that plough up and down the channel). On occasions we would tow a barrage balloon from our after bollards. It must have been a strange sight for some of the merchant ships and especially for passengers on the liners.

As the anti-submarine teams on the frigates gained expertise, so the complexity of the 'hunt the submarine' games increased and we would be using the full extent of the exercise areas. We might be avoiding two or three frigates coming in to attack and often flooding 'Q' tank at the last minute, it seemed, to get to a safe depth. Their sharp bow travelling at 25 to 30 knots would open us up like a sardine can. The sound of their screws and pounding of their engines as they crossed our overhead was often followed by explosive charges to signify their attack – the noise those small charges made was only a taster for what a real anti-submarine mortar's bomb would sound like.

It was during one of these attacks that our sister, the Thule was severely damaged by the fleet oiler 'Black Ranger' on the 18 November 1960. (If you look up H.M. submarine Thule on the internet you can view the Pathe news item taken when she returned to Gosport). That was close to being another disaster. The Thule had to be scrapped as a result.

Shortly after I left the Tiptoe she was struck by the frigate 'Yarmouth' about 10 miles southeast of Portland Bill. I've always said we were in much more danger from our own Navy than from that of the Russians.

Tiptoe was also lucky to survive but at least she managed to inflict considerable damage on her opponent the Yarmouth. I met a former baby stoker (as he described himself) at my brother's golden wedding celebration recently. He told me Yarmouth was his first ship and he was afraid they would sink as the forward compartments were flooded and the ship was listing to starboard.

Often we were 'day running'. This meant that every day we ourselves became well practiced at routines such as 'harbour station for entering and leaving harbour', 'opening up for diving', 'diving on the klaxon' and coming up to the surface again, amid the busy shipping of the channel. This kept the sonar operators on their toes, trying to help the captain determine the position of these vessels, relative to the patch of water we wanted to emerge from.

At times, if the day's games finished late and before the next day's games were due to start, the skipper would sit us on the sandy bottom, to allow all but a few watchkeepers to get a night's sleep. This needed to be achieved with care, to avoid striking the bottom with force and also keeping the screws and rudder clear of any potentially fouling debris. At the time I thought the captain was an expert at this but looking back I now think that as he was then only a two ringer (lieutenant) aboard his first boat as skipper it could well have been his first attempt. The art, it seemed, was to descend slowly, after using the echo-sounder, with a slight bow down angle. Once the bow grounded the trim would be adjusted to keep the bow heavy and the stern light, to keep us in position. It was an unusual experience to lay in my bunk close to the bow, with the absence of the usual noises of the submarine under way and feel and hear the movement as the current slewed us about, but overall it would be peaceful.

Arriving back in Portland we moored at the inshore end of the jetty, the bow pointing toward the shoreline which was only about fifty yards away. A number of the crew, taking advantage of the boat's self mainte-nance period, went on a few days leave amongst them the T.I. (Torpedo Instructor, a Petty Officer) and Deaks the killik torpedoman. During this period, for calibration purposes, air shots were fired from the forrard torpedo tubes. Exactly why this was being done I wasn't sure not being a torpedoman myself. Apart from sleeping next to reloads and airing my socks atop their warheads (my socks, the only item of clothing apart from my steaming boots that I would remove before zipping myself into my quick release sleeping bag) – I didn't get too involved with them although sometimes I had to assist steadying torpedoes being lifted by crane from a jetty or depot ship and helping to guide them through the loading hatch and onto the rails. I quite happily strove within the at-tack team to get us into a good attacking position so they could fire the beastly things. When checking through the boat as trot sentry, I would open the drain cock of the rear door of any unloaded tube and push the reamer through to ensure the drain cock wasn't blocked and that the tube was indeed dry as it should be.

Since the 'Thetis' disaster, when the drain cock had negligently been blocked with congealed paint by a shipyard workman, lessons had been learned. A Thetis clip, as we called it, was fitted to prevent the rear door being opened fully should an amalgamation of errors and bad workman-ship, that which caused the loss of Thetis the first of the 'T' class, result-ing in the largest loss of life in British submarine history.

I had to learn of the various water tanks involved with torpedo opera-tions to pass my Part 3 training before gaining my submarine badge. Obviously a torpedo is loaded into an empty tube, once the rear door is shut, the W.R.T. (water round torpedoes) tank provides water to fill the space while the air it replaces is vented inboard, then again this tank is used to drain down the tube after use.

The torpedo operating tank, empty when the submarine is loaded with torpedoes is filled as they are fired to compensate the loss of their weight or we would pretty soon pop to the surface bows upwards did we not do so. On firing, the torpedo is forced from the tube by H.P. air, its propulsion machine will only kick in once the 'fish' is moving through the water. This H.P. air mixed with some water is captured through automatic inboard vents into an open topped tank to prevent it escaping to create a tell-tale disturbance at the surface.

You are now as wise as me, but anyway by now Deaks has returned from leave and has enquired about the two fish that were loaded in two of the tubes. After some scratching of heads it was realised that along with air shots two fish were now reposing on the harbour floor. Luckily they were not armed with warheads and set up ready to run or our watering hole, the Breakwater Bar, would surely have pulled its last pint.

I think these fish must have been recovered on the Q.T. as heads did not roll; they probably as usual blamed the subby (sub-lieutenant, the most junior officer). It was never discovered who had removed the boards which hung over the rear door of a loaded tube.

Buoy Jumper

When Budgie received his draft to join a newly built submarine I asked the scratcher if I could take Budgie's place as scratchers dickie. Budgie was a legend among submariners. He was a man mountain with biceps the size of an average man's thighs. Once while I was working on deck with him, we watched a couple of stokers struggling to carry a replacement main engine piston from the jetty, over the gangway, around the bridge structure and down the engine room hatch. The two of them made hard work of it. "Bloody bilge rats" said Budgie. He picked up one of the pistons from the jetty, steadied it over his shoulder, kept one hand free to pull himself up the gangplank and to steady himself around the bridge, then he lowered it down the engine room hatch to whoever was below. All the while he was doing it, Budgie was berating the oilys. If they took offence they never showed it to Budgie. Mind you he was a very easy going fellow and hard to upset.

The scratcher, or second coxswain to give him his proper title, was in charge of all upper deck operations. He worked under the direction of the torpedo officer who had ultimate responsibility. These duties included anything to do with mooring, i.e. ropes and wires, anchors and cables, towing. Also when we carried out special operations like launching special forces in small boat operations and helicopter transfers of personnel, mail and stores. He had an assistant known in naval parlance as his 'dickie'. One of the duties of scratchers dickie was to act as buoy jumper. Buoy jumping done on a calm summer's day was pleasant and fun and fairly routine.

A submarine, unlike a surface warship carries no launches with which to transfer the buoy jumper. Instead the captain has to manouvre the submarine up to the buoy, heading into the wind and tide so as not to overrun it. The buoy jumper, i.e. me, has to jump onto the buoy attached to a line to pass the picking-up rope and ultimately to secure the ship-to-buoy shackle.

I had carried out this operation a few times in calm and not so calm weather with no problem. My sternest test was yet to come. First, let me explain that a mooring buoy is nothing like the landlubber might see in his local yacht harbour. It is large enough to moor a ship the size of a battleship, aircraft carrier or passenger liner and is securely anchored to the seabed. All of the ones I have 'jumped' are the shape of a round metal drum, although there are some that have a flat surface which are probably easier to get a foothold on.

This particular time I had an added pressure. I think it was at Rothesay, Isle of Bute, we had about twenty of the crew waiting down in the fore-ends, weekend bags packed. Their wives and girlfriends having traveled from wherever for a long weekend break.

The night was pitch black, sleety snow swirling in the squall. The captain said he would make a couple of attempts to pick up the buoy and if not successful we would lie off in shelter somewhere overnight and try again when the weather moderated the next day.

I stood on the bulbous bow close to the bullring. I was attached to a lifeline tended by the scratcher. I was trembling from the cold and tension but also from fear. Not fear of jumping onto the buoy but fear of failure on my part. I don't suppose any of those waiting down below would relish changing places with me, but they were probably wishing it was Budgie up there in my place.

As we neared the buoy and could use it as a reference point, it emphasised the rise and fall of the bow. The skipper was jockeying with the main motors and helm to bring our bow close to the buoy, the thought of falling between the two didn't bear considering.

Suddenly we were close and I thought it's now or never – I hurled myself at the buoy just as scratcher yelled "Don't jump". Too late, I landed on the buoy, lunged at the buoy ring and got a handhold at the same time as the submarine, with main motors going full astern, struck the buoy causing it to spin wildly. That didn't bother me now that I was here. I could stand the discomfort, my tension and fear were gone, securing the picking up rope and then the shackle my only goal. How they got me off the buoy would be their problem, along with the problem of transferring weekenders to an MFV.

As they hauled me back aboard and I made my way below it was the first time I had received accolades from my shipmates. It was a good feeling, as it was when the captain approved a rum issue for the casing crew.

A whale of a time
in Campbeltown

A whale of a time in Campbeltown

The silence was golden, the sun warming the still surface of Campbeltown Loch. The temperatures here are above average for the UK as it is close to the gulf stream. Perhaps the whale was here for that reason.

I was alone on deck, the submarine being moored to an old wooden jetty. In its heyday this beautiful sheltered harbour would have been alive with fishing boats and with other boats being built. Today, the fishing season being good, the remaining fishing boats were all out, reaping the harvest of mackerel, whiting, pollock and probably lobster. Had they been in harbour and unloading their catch, the silence would have been shattered by the squealing and wailing of herring gulls in their hordes.

Although by no means am I a 'twitcher' I have always enjoyed watching birds, especially when they are hunting their food. Today I was watching occasional groups of guillemots or razorbills. I couldn't always tell the difference unless they were close enough for me to see their bills. There would be kittiwakes and terns, but not in noisy hordes, and the usual Mother Carey's chickens, as we termed the petrels. From the casing I could look at the hills over which I had clambered the day previous. I had crossed the shingle causeway to Davaar Island at low tide, but not stayed there long, as the tide was beginning to turn and

I was due back on board. I could hear an aircraft noise and then as it climbed above the hills, I could see an Orion maritime patrol aircraft which had taken off from RAF Machriahanish. No doubt it was off to hunt for Soviet submarines or perhaps to play with one of ours, but that was far from my mind on this peaceful day.

While we were at the jetty the First Lieutenant had taken the opportunity for us, his foot soldiers, to re-paint the ballast tanks and casing to replace the paint that angry seas had stripped from them.

This Jimmy was a very pleasant independent minded soul who, I understand, went on to make admiral, after various commands including a nuclear missile firing submarine and a major surface ship during the Falklands campaign. His brilliant theory was, if once we had applied the thick brown/black undercoat and allowed it to get tacky and we then painted on the shiny black topcoat, the sea would, in future, not take our paint. So we stood on the curved ballast tanks and with our long toms, painted them and the sides of the casing as we worked our way aft. By the time we'd finished we judged that the paint near the bow was just right for the topcoat, which we applied with long handled rollers, working our way toward the stern while standing on the tacky undercoat. We spent a couple of hours sitting on the jetty cleaning paint off ourselves while admiring our artwork. Being upwardly mobile and a star, the Jimmy wasn't around long enough to savour the fruits of our labours. The next Jimmy would probably favour some other application method and we would nod and give him the impression he was saving the world.

We had been granted a 'make and mend' today which allowed those not on duty to get away early for weekend leave. I had elected to do the afternoon stint as sentry, up on the casing, as the rest of the duty watch wanted to watch some programme on our newly acquired black and white TV down below in the forrard mess.

They were obviously not getting a good signal, as every so often someone would come up to adjust the ramshackle aerial, shouting down the hatch to those below to check picture quality. They must have been satisfied eventually, as he disappeared below. Tranquility returned and soon I was in a world of my own.

All of a sudden as I gazed into the calm waters the humped back of a large whale broke surface, right alongside where I stood, about six feet away from me. The whale blew a gushing spout of water into the air before disappearing back into the depths of the loch. My shouts down the hatch brought the lads up top, although the whale was long gone, the evidence to back up my story was dripping off me and off the casing and their carefully adjusted aerial was on its side.

Anticipation

My grandson is going to be banished to an outhouse I'm building in the back garden, well I'm not actually doing the brickying and chippying, just the organizing. It made me think of sound powered telephones, a good method of communicating with him and of waking him up. I haven't seen one since the Navy. We used them on the submarines, one place in particular was between the fore-ends and the control room. One of its most frequent usages was when one took a dump in the forward W.C. (the six position flap valve, individual discharge to sea). The depositer would usually shout to the forendsman who would spin the phone's handle which generated the power and alerted the control room messenger, who would take the call and relate the message to the officer of the watch.

Apart from answering this phone the messenger would be standing beside the helmsman who sat on a seat in front of the steering position with its wheel (which was usually not a wheel, but a hydraulic tapper bar, on all but the older 'T' boats on which I'd served), the gyro compass repeater and the engine, main motor and grouper telegraphs. The messenger would operate the various telegraphs as ordered, leaving the helmsman free to concentrate on steering. While doing these tasks he also kept the control room log up to date, as every order, every depth change, alteration of course, incident – the lot, had to be logged to the nearest quarter minute. Sometimes he was scribbling furiously as orders came thick and fast, at other times when perhaps the submarine was mooching about at 150ft, at slow speed, steady course and in good trim, his pencil would be still. I don't know how long the Navy keeps these completed log books, but they must have enough to fill the Albert Hall ten times over.

During one particular quiet time, our double barrel named son of an army brigadier, thickset, rugby scrum-half type, torpedo officer, was officer of the watch. I was on the foreplanes which I liked, being one of the submarine service's finest foreplanesmen. It was all about anticipation and my life was full of that – normally unfulfilled – and more hope than anticipation if the truth be known. You watch the bubble sus' out its next movement put on a little dive or rise, keeping the depth gauge needle spot on. No problem at 150ft where movement is limited, but at 45ft in the troughs and crests of ten to fifteen foot rollers perhaps and the need for the eyes at the periscope to be all seeing without being all showing, could be a different matter. One hour was the limit of concentration, for even the service's best.

The messenger was able seaman Browski. We called him 'Louie' or 'Dumb' (a play on Louie Dumbrowski of the Bowery Boys films, which I used to watch at the Tilbury bug hutch on Saturday mornings as a kid). Now the scene was set, the right actors in place for Deaks to pull one of his stunts, because he knew Louie, not being what you would call a quick thinker, would pass on exactly what he heard from the other end of the sound powered, wind-up telephone, to the officer of the watch.

Deaks went forrard for a dump and after his deposit rang the phone. He requested permission to "Fire a shit shot from forrard". This was not an unusual way for the depositer to request this, but normally the messenger would translate it to the regulation "Permission to blow the forrard heads, sir". Not so Dumb Browski. For all of this officer's outward appearance, he was rather staid, God fearing and without any perceptible humour, but had a fiery temper and a short fuse. I concentrated on my depth gauge and tried to stop my shoulders shaking with the laughter that I sought to suppress, as the officer of the watch stood right behind me. The rest of the control room crew were similarly engaged, but the E.R.A. (engine room artificer) on the blowing panel couldn't control his snorts of laughter and soon we were all at it. Poor Dumb Browski, he wouldn't hurt a fly himself.

Stand by for gun action

I thought describing the outline of the procedure for gun action interesting for some as it is now consigned to history. I served on the last 'T' and the last 'A' class fitted with the 4" gun and both after the Indonesian campaign when a number of streamlined 'A' class as well as a few Porpoise and Oberon class had a 4" deck gun or one of a lighter calibre fitted temporarily. Perhaps it was coincidence that I served on the last of each class to have the permanent mounting.

We were one of the Group 2 'T' Class boats built with a riveted hull and as such were not suitable for conversion as were the Group 3 welded hull boats. We therefore retained the 4" quick firing gun, fitted just forward of our bridge. In the Navy, if you have it you train to use it, even though the likelihood of ever having to use the gun in anger was extremely remote.

Most of our submarines carried only one rating of the gunnery branch, all the ones I'd met were gunlayers by specialization. The gunlayer looked after the gun and its ammunition. He also looked after the stens or lanchester carbines, hand grenades, pistols and grenade pistols we carried to defend the submarine or arm boarding parties with. He also looked after the line throwing rifle.

When a target had been identified by periscope, the order "Stand by for gun action" would be made. The gunlayer followed by his four gun crew members would man the guntower. The four ammunition supply members would have the magazine hatch open and be standing by to pass the projectiles up to the crew. The gunlayer removes the pins to the clips of his hatch. The surfacing officer removes the pins to the clips of the conning tower hatch, following him up the ladder will be the armament officer and the surfacing lookout.

The intention is to surface as quickly as possible and get the projectiles away, hopefully on target, before whoever you are firing at has time to react and return fire. Although this is a practice, the first lieutenant is standing by in the Control Room with a stopwatch to take timings. At the order "Surface", main ballast tanks are blown, the submarine is held down initially with hydroplanes 'hard to dive' then the planes are reversed to 'hard to rise'.

When the boat reaches about 25ft the first lieutenant blows his whistle which is the order to open both hatches. The crew mans the gun and trains onto the target. The original range had been worked out from the periscope and the 'fruit machine' (which is what we called the torpedo control system-submarines). Once the armament officer was on the bridge he would make adjustments to the range and deflection, according to his binocular observations. 'The flash, the crash, the smoke and the smell as back comes the gun and away goes the shell'. The shoot completed the gun is secured in preparation for diving.

If the order "Down below" was given this signified an emergency, the gun would be abandoned the crew had to get below and shut the hatch. No doubt in this situation the klaxon would have sounded twice causing the submarine to dive instantly.

Being radar plot specialisation I would not be in the guns crew, but if not required to operate the radar set, or one of the plots, I could be used for ammo supply. Quite often the chef, steward and tanky would be used as gun crew as they were not watchkeepers or in the attack team. It may surprise the reader to learn this but chef and steward were just as much submariners as the rest of us and in fact I've served with two stewards in particular who were among the finest.

Coincidence

Another coincidence occurred as I was writing the 'Stand By For Gun Action' chapter. Answering our phone my wife heard a voice at the other end say "Admiralty calling". She immediately recognized the Bristolian accent – it was former submarine gunlayer Peter Burnett. We hadn't spoken to him for several years.

It was many years after leaving the Navy that I met Pete. I was in Cyprus with my daughter Jayne. Our family usually went to our apartment in Protaras for an early season holiday and I went out again toward the end of October to tie up leases for the following year, as we had a small holiday business there.

The first evening of our stay we called in at La Paz bar, at the far end of the town from our apartment, we were friendly with Adam the owner. Seeing me enter Adam poured me a good measure of Pussers rum. It was early evening and the bar was empty apart from a big handsome, suntanned fellow, a similar age to me or perhaps slightly older. With him was an attractive younger woman, laughing and joking with him, but I didn't draw any conclusion from that.

The man called out "You kept the Pussers hidden Adam, I fancy a proper tot myself". It was the way he said it that made me ask "You been in the Andrew mate?" Then coincidences flowed thick and fast as first he introduced his daughter Nikki. He said he had a second daughter Lynn and she lived in Chelmsford which is about 15 minutes from our home. Yes, he is ex-RN he said, trained at St Vincent and in Anson Division the same as myself. He served on one general service ship and then volunteered for submarines.

When I asked where he was staying he said "Up the other end of Protaras behind Rocks Restaurant". He told me he leased a house there where he and his wife Rene could stay a few months each year for health reasons. I could look over the balcony from our apartment, down the hill, and see his house. The owner of Rocks, Adam, is the uncle of Adam of La Paz and has been our friend for many years.

As regards Pete's health, Rene describes him as a creaking door, but to me he's like one of Anson's square rigged ships on a following sea, with masts and yards creaking and groaning, but pressing on regardless. He's the healthiest looking unhealthy person I've ever seen. He still manages to bear the standard at HMS St Vincent association and remembrance parades.

Personal hygiene and domestic chores

Space on board was at a premium as every nook and cranny would be filled with essential stores and spare gear, uniform and kit having a low priority. I had parted company with most of mine since joining submarines. Somebody somewhere is probably swinging in my hammock. Gone is the tin hatbox as is the leather edged green canvas covered good quality suitcase in favour of the pussers grip – the brown zip-up bag you would see matelots clutching as they zoomed ashore on weekend leave. If somebody started a gas attack I would have to stick my head under the blankets as I had chucked the gas mask out of my kitbag to make room for something of more immediate use. It's the main reason I think that many submariners didn't revert back to general service once the five year period they had volunteered for expired.

What we did have though was a small kit locker about 2ft x 18ins x 18ins. The trouble with it was it would be located in the mess underneath the cushion of whoever had the bottom bunk, or used as a seat at mealtimes by those around the mess table. You could upset people if you kept wanting to go to it. I tended to keep any items I wanted as ready use like my current reading material, toothpaste and brush and spare socks zipped up under my bunk cushion.

Our going ashore uniform, our No. 1's, would only be brought with us if we were calling at a port where shore leave could be granted, otherwise it was left at the base or on the depot ship. If we had it with us a hanging wire would be rigged in the port after end of the fore-ends. We would put it on a hanger, our Burberry on top and the lot covered with a plastic cover. Our Burberry raincoat was all purpose, a warm lining could be zipped in, or it could double as a groundsheet, for certain events!

For leaving and entering harbour us seamen would wear working dress trousers and white submarine sweater, or smock in pusser's terms, with lifebelt over. Once we'd done our thing with the mooring ropes and wires or the anchor and cable we would form a little ceremonial line on the fore casing and 'those' on bridge would salute the flag of the base or of any senior officers ship we passed while the 'bunting tosser' sounded the still on his bosuns call.

We would trot off below before exiting the harbour entrance and then change into what we called steaming rig which we would wear for the remainder of the voyage. This would be a mish mash of uniform or civvie clothing, whatever we found comfortable. Once when being filmed doing gun actions for the movie 'Sea Wolves' we were issued with German Navy combat jackets and forage caps. Some of us used it as steaming rig until it eventually disintegrated.

We had no facilities for showering or bathing and had limited fresh water, the fresh water tanks and the amount our distiller produced would only be enough for drinking and cooking purposes. We had just two stainless steel handbasins so we could at least wash our hands, faces and of course clean our teeth.

The only item of kit I washed at sea were the thin nylon socks that I wore inside my pull-on steaming boots. Thin because they needed to be quick drying, either hung in front of a ventilation punka louvre or draped over the water boiler which we used for making our mugs of tea or ki. This would be permanently fogging away next to our mess doorway (or where the door would have been if we had one). Only the captain's cabin and the wardroom had a door – us peons, the great unwashed, needed no privacy.

Sometimes when on a flag showing trip at a UK or foreign port the boat would be open for visitors. It was like being in a zoo cage as a continuous line of visitors filed past. Some would ask really interesting questions like "Does this submarine ever go under water?" or "Have you got any portholes?". One dear sweet old lady, well she was probably in her fifties but being like twenty myself that would seem old, she quite seriously asked me where we did our shopping and did we get newspapers. I said well the coxswain is also known as the grocer and yes we did get the newspapers but they were usually about six weeks out of date.

We did take a pride in our little 'home from home' and each evening we would break out a few bits of rag from the bale that the scratcher kept in his little caboosh and we would wipe through the accommodation space and control room flooring with white spirit. This helped to remove the oily film that was trodden through daily. The white spirit odour added to the piquancy of other smells that permeated our atmosphere.

We of the lower order each had a cleaning station where we could show off our domestic skills. On this boat mine was the Seamen's Bathroom as it was called although it had no bath, only the two handbasins. Also directly opposite on the other side of the passageway I cleaned the Officers Bathroom. Being gentry they had a door so they could perform their ablutions in private. It was while doing my cleaning chores that most mornings I would be greeted by our double-barrel named, son of an army brigadier, torpedo officer, the one that looked like a rugby scrum half. He would trot out of the wardroom clad in a short dark blue toweling dressing gown, his towel folded over his arm and clutching his small shaving bag. You would think he was at Claridges of Mayfair. "Just going for my morning George" he would say in passing. The saying must have rubbed off on me as I use it to this day, much to the amusement of my grandson. Another tribute to our officers who led by example.

Talking of this gallant officer who I looked up to during the two years we served together, he being over six foot and me a mere five foot nine, he never mastered the gentle art of maintaining the trim. I could sometimes tell, while lying in my bunk, that he was officer of the watch by the arse down, bow up, attitude that the boat had – not to change depth, just to plod on level at 200ft or so. I liked to be on the foreplanes during his watch where I could test my mettle.

I've never been a horseman, apart from a couple of donkey rides at the seaside, or once or twice when we invested the few bob we earned delivering Daily Mirrors, Sketches and the News of the Screws from Mr Harvey's paper shop, on one of the riding nags at Sticking's Farm, more because we fancied the riding pants off Molly Stickings than for any love of horseflesh. We often rode pretend horses as kids having just watched a Roy Rogers, Hopalong Cassidy or Gene Autry film, some Saturday mornings at Tilbury's bug hutch movie theatre. We used to ride one handed, holding the reins in one hand and smacking the backs of the top of our thighs with the other, all the time making clacking sounds through our teeth to simulate horses' hoofs. Most boys had it off to a tee.

This though, on the foreplanes, with our torpedo officer on the trim, could be like riding a bucking bronco, or taking the jumps at Aintree on the back of a porpoise. One could raise a sweat under pack ice, doing a one hour stint trying to iron out the bumps even on the calmest of days. Whether it was because the captain liked him as a person, or saw some potential that was obscure to us, the hoi polloi, that he never got reverted to general service as did some officers or other grades, who for some reason didn't measure up in some way. He was often the subject of the yarns we would spin, when together in a bar with crew members of other submarines. They would tell of quirky officers or others they'd served with.

I told them a true story of one time that I was surfacing look-out about to follow 'Torps' out of the tower once we broke surface. The call came up from below "Pressure in the boat". Now sometimes the captain would order the blower to be run to reduce this excess pressure which had built up inside the hull. One cause of this could be much use of the 'Q' 'rapid getting down to a safe depth tank' to clear approaching surface ships and the subsequent venting inboard of the high pressure air, used to blow the ballast water out, afterwards.

This time instead of running the L.P. blower he relied on the surfacing officer, Torps, to allow the excess air pressure to bleed out by just cracking the tower hatch clips, but holding them on their safety lugs. Not so our gallant torpedo officer, he just swung open the clips and took off in the rush of the suddenly released air. Like Yuri Gagarin aboard Vostok 1, he would have ended up in orbit but for the periscope standards coming into contact with the white top of his 'U' boat commander style cap that he wore at a rakish angle.

Like the good surfacing lookout that I purported to be, upon hearing the precautionary advice "Pressure in the boat" I had wrapped my arms around Torps' long sea boots and entwined my legs around the tower ladder. I was left clinging to his empty loose fitting sea boots as he went out like a champagne cork from a shaken bottle. Now to give Torps his due after shaking his head a bit, his Dartmouth[1] training kicked in, he leant down to the voice pipe whose shut-off cock I had just opened, and gave the helmsman a course to steer, before donning the sea boots I handed him.

Torps was full of the 'bulldog spirit' which Churchill had used to prize open the coffers of our American cousins at the beginning of WWII. Better a rousing speech than "Give us your old destroyers and we'll show you how to use them". Press on regardless was Torps modus operandi – probably why the captain liked him.

---

[1]Royal Naval College, Dartmouth, Devon, established 1863, motto 'to deliver courageous leaders with the spirit to fight and win'.

Sandown / Shanklin Regatta

Every so often boats from the first submarine squadron based at HMS Dolphin, Gosport, would be sent on a visit, as a break, to a port somewhere perhaps on the west coast of France or to one of the Channel Islands or even northern Spain. We were sent across the Solent to act as guardship for the Sandown/Shanklin Regatta.

A submarine is not much of a guard ship. We didn't even have a boat to take our own liberty men ashore, or to take the R.A's[1] back to Gosport where their families were living in married quarters. We were there to show the flag, to take part in the shoreside celebrations and to give us a break.

---

[1] When an R.N. vessel is at her home port the married men whose families were in the vicinity would not be victualed on board, but would get a ration allowance to live ashore. Thus they were known as R.A.s

I remember in the afternoons our soccer team would play in the knockout competition. After our tug of war team lost things got boisterous, we tossed our opponents off the pier to the delight of the spectators, we tossed the referee in and then we chucked ourselves over the railings to join them in the water.

An MFV was sent over from the dockyard to take us ashore in the evening. The MFV was scheduled to pick up returning liberty men at 2300hrs and at 0030hrs from the pier. A crowd of us went ashore together and then as usually happens people drift off for one reason or another. I ended up with just my regular run ashore oppo 'Smudger'. He was Canadian Navy, the original 'wild colonial boy'. He never wanted to give up, I think he feared prohibition would be declared at any time soon.

Just to explain, most of our submarines had two or three Canadians in the crew and possibly a similar number of Australians. We had a squadron in each of those countries. They both had a number of the new 'Oberon' class boats on order from our shipyards and were training up crews to man them and to form their own submarine arms. The Canadian Government really looked after their servicemen. They were given a monthly spirit allowance and plenty of cigarettes they could barter with. At Christmas gifts were sent down to them from their London headquarters. Quite a few of their men were ex-R.N. who had transferred over at the end of their R.N. service, something to do with the film star pay perhaps.

Anyway I have veered off course. By the time Smudger and I found our way back to the pier we'd missed the boat. At some places we'd been to the liberty boat would tie up to the pier or jetty and its crew would get their heads down until the first trip was due next morning, so we would be able to kip down also. Not so here, they went back to pompey and their own beds. Sandy beaches shimmer in the sunshine, but at night with an onshore breeze blowing our teeth were soon chattering. We could see the anchor lights of our floating hotel about a mile offshore.

I don't recall how we discovered it, but some of the securing chains of the pedalos were only looped over. Full of Dutch courage and the warmth of our bunks beckoning it was hard to resist. We soon had one of the craft in the water and set course, pedaling like men possessed. We made good progress but once out in the bay we were fighting the tide and sobering up fast. We feared making landfall in Normandy or even the eastern seaboard of the U.S.

After furious legwork and fit to collapse we were close enough to hail the anchor watchman on the bridge. He told us the next day that he could hardly believe his ears when our yells came out of the blackness. We caught the heaving line he threw and were soon alongside and scrambling up onto the casing. Between the three of us we managed to pull the pedalo inboard. We said we would take it back on the MFV in the morning.

I was asleep as soon as I hit my bunk. It was a couple of hours later when the Duty Officer emerged onto the bridge to check the anchor bearings that he noticed the pedalo – well he could hardly miss it – it was bright yellow. The Captain was due back aboard in the morning on the first boat from Gosport. Fearing his wrath, the Duty Officer summoned us from our slumbers and told us to pedal it back ashore. Luckily we had the wind and tide in our favour but we had to wait about three hours for the morning liberty boat.

I've detested pedalos since that time!

Augur at the movies

It was not like a night on Broadway or around the Haymarket and Tottenham Court Road. No red carpet, no ice cream, popcorn, or usherette. What we did have though was a selection of movies even though we were at the mercy of the taste of whoever had gone to the Naval Film Library to choose them in the first place. A poor choice could mean that after we had suffered them it would be difficult to swap them with a good film from any ship or submarine we might encounter on our travels.

Usually we had something watchable, a main feature film – a shit-kicker (as we called a cowboy/western) or a Cary Grant, Doris Day, Rock Hudson type of thing, usually preceded by a Tom and Jerry, Bugs Bunny, or some other short cartoon, a bit of escapism from our dreary routine.

With the permission of the Jimmy we, of the forrard mess, would rig up the little projector in the fore-ends somewhere below the fore hatch so it could project its beam onto the 4ft x 4ft screen suspended from the deckhead between the tube space doors. The lucky ones of the audience would sit on one of the bench lockers which had a vinyl cushion atop it. The not so lucky would squat where they could, as long as their heads were clear of the beam, otherwise they would suffer abuse from all and sundry.

If we happened to be on the surface some of the engine room staff might come forward to join us. Whenever dived, anyone going either forward or aft of the control room was required to ask permission of the officer of the watch. He would normally answer "Yes please, yes please" a few times until his built in calculator told him that a disproportionate number had moved in one direction or the other, enough to affect the fore and aft balance. He would stop any more movement until some from whichever was the heavier end had gone the opposite way. This would save a lot of unnecessary pumping and flooding to adjust what was probably a good trim in the first place.

The P.O.'s mess would show their choice of movie another evening. The projector would be set up on their mess table to shine its beam across the passageway outside and onto the screen suspended from the curtain rail of the top bunk on the far side of the 3ft wide passageway. Anyone wishing to move fore or aft would have to duck down under the beam and avoid the legs of those squatting in the passageway to watch the P.O's film.

Escapism was easier to achieve when we were dived and not putting on too great an angle when changing depth. Not so easy to get lost in another world when our world was rocking and rolling on the surface. Wherever the movie was shown, it could suffer from the same disruptions – the film itself could break, as could the projector, or its bulb could blow. The Jimmy wouldn't have given permission if we were expecting to go to 'diving' or 'attack' stations – but in our little world the unexpected had a habit of rearing its head – all part of the fun. "If you can't take a joke you shouldn't have joined", as the wise one would point out.

A Whale of a time in The Irish Sea

We were somewhere in the Irish Sea which was not one of our usual stomping grounds. We were at 'watch diving' which meant two thirds of the crew would be in their bunks as it was the middle of the night. I always chose a bunk in the fore-ends (the torpedo loading compartment). In fact, whatever submarine I was on I never had a bunk either in the mess or in the passageway. Each area had disadvantages. I didn't fancy the passageway even though the bunks there were a permanent fixture. Being the only thoroughfare it was akin to living on a main road as those going on and off watch had to pass through. It was too narrow for two people to pass each other without leaning into the curtain which gave the sleeping occupant his only semblance of privacy. This was even worse when the boat was rolling or pitching about.

In the mess the bottom bunks doubled as seats at mealtimes or during card games, the top bunks were lowered off their chains to form the backrests. Another big disadvantage to having a bunk in the mess was that whenever access was required to maintain the batteries, in their tanks under the deck, the whole mess furniture had to be stripped out.

Where I chose to sleep, the fore-ends, housed eighteen bunks, nine each side, three sets of three, suspended from chains when in their raised position. This allowed a couple of feet between each bunk. Between the bunks and the curved sides of the hull were stowed the reload torpedoes. Each was the length of the three sets of bunks. They could either be fitted with warheads containing 200lbs of TNT, or with blowing heads which allowed the expensive weapon to be recovered, when fired during practice attacks.

If I could, I would opt for the top bunk in one of the centre or forward tiers, even though it suffered more from the condensation dripping off the curved steel pressure hull just above. (It didn't pay to contemplate the number of fathoms between it and the ocean's surface.) At least in the top bunk I didn't suffer anyone's feet dangling over from above.

The after set of bunks were either side of the fore hatch. This hatch was angled to allow torpedoes to be brought aboard the submarine when in harbour. Also in harbour the main access ladder was rigged. If you can picture Jolly Jack Tar returning half cut from his run ashore, either falling through the hatch, or just waking up the bunks' occupants to tell them what good chaps he thought they were – or worse throwing up his beer and chips over them! The main disadvantage of being in the fore-ends was when the torpedo tubes had to be reloaded and all the bunks had to be dismantled. Still as the saying goes, "If you can't take a joke you shouldn't have joined".

Anyway I have digressed. We were down at 300ft and making about 4 knots, an economical speed to conserve battery power. From that speed to a sudden dead stop had a massive effect, waking those asleep and causing some bumps and bruises to those on watch.

We surfaced in pretty quick time, the Captain not knowing what we had struck or if we had sustained damage, didn't want to be at 300ft when he found out. Once on the surface we could see no evidence of damage, so it was doubtful we'd had a chance collision with another submarine or snagged the nets of a fishing vessel. We criss-crossed the area using echo sounder but could find no evidence of an uncharted rock pinnacle. The only logical conclusion was that we had encountered a large whale, although we could find no evidence of that either.

A briefcase of orders
and a game of uckers

'Mystery Tours' or 'Sneakies', are the submariners term for patrols into areas which are close to, or inside, other countries territorial waters. They weren't spoken about in any depth outside of one's own crew. Since the 'Iron Curtain' descended a cold war had existed between NATO and the Warsaw Pact. Relations between the West and the Soviets had become even icier since the Buster Crabbe affair and the shooting down of the U2 spyplane piloted by Gary Powers in 1960, and a second one over the Barents sea a couple of month later. Submarines possessed the stealth and endurance to carry out surveillance of the Soviet fleet and shore installations. Any submarine caught inside Soviet waters would expect to be attacked.

Unlike ships of the merchant marine that used the well-worn paths of the shipping lanes, heading toward a beacon of light, defined headlands and harbours, the Statue of Liberty, Sydney Harbour Bridge, the Angel overlooking Rio, Table Mountain and Cape of Good Hope, our objective was to reach a precise patrol position marked on the chart of a northern gale swept ocean, ordered by staff officers working somewhere in an underground bunker operations room.

The boat would've been prepared for the patrol spending time in the floating dock and she would be stored with extra food, mainly tinned, and with other essential spares The need was to be self-contained and self-maintained as there would be little likelihood of outside help in the event of mechanical breakdown or running aground. Any dire medical emergency would mean withdrawal to the closest NATO coastline, probably Norway or even Iceland, to carry out a helicopter transfer, otherwise the patient would be left to the tender mercy of the coxswain.

The white NATO identification numbers would be painted over with black, even though the total patrol would be carried out submerged. Half a dozen 'new faces' appeared among the crew, some were specialists from Whitehall, Russian speakers, who would work in the wireless office, others set up recording equipment which would tape all transmission detected through our various listening devices. This increase in crew numbers meant 'hot bunking' for those that slept in the passageway and messes. This meant that an off coming watch member would move his sleeping bag into the bunk of a person going on watch. It didn't affect those that slept in the fore-ends but they had an extra inconvenience of a false deck of supplies to clamber over.

Liberty men might return at 2330hrs to ready for harbour stations at 0100hrs. Those married men having said their goodbyes, leaving children asleep in bed and wives to cope alone unsure of her husband's whereabouts for the next six weeks or so. The captain would usually arrive last, holding a briefcase containing orders, say his farewell to the staff officer at the gangway of the depot ship, return the salute of our casing crew as he crossed the gangplank which would be pulled in and stowed as he was climbing up to the bridge. The first lieutenant would report "Submarine ready for sea" as all checks would have been carried out prior to the captain's arrival. Heading off into the teeth of a gale at some unearthly hour would be seen as a norm. A tide, perhaps, may affect departure but weather and time would not - with the exception of a hurricane.

Within sight of land one could hope for a good navigation fix on known points of land, light beacons or buoys – visibility allowing. In those days, before inertial satellite navigation, taking a star sight using sextant through the periscope might be the only option, cloudless night sky permitting, once away from land. The navigator and captain would often be in a huddle over the chart table in the gloom of the dim red lit control room. A cynic might say it was by guess and by God, but it was a testimony to their skill to arrive on time and on track.

Murmansk on the Kola peninsula, protected by the Gulf stream, is Russia's only year round ice free port, the others need ice breakers to clear shipping channels. For their ships and submarines to enter the Atlantic they would pass around northern Norway and through the Iceland gap. Stationing NATO submarines in the Barents sea and along that route would enable surveillance on their movements and intelligence gathering closer in to the Pechanga naval base and the Kola peninsula with its mass of military installations which included an estimated forty military airfields.

Whichever patrol area, any vessel encountered would be regarded as hostile, even fishing boats which were not always what they seemed. Snorting had to be carried out during the darkest hours in the remotest part of the area to avoid revealing the submarine's presence, so for the duration of the patrol effectively night was turned into day. While the noisy diesels were in use to generate power for the batteries any essential maintenance was carried out, as was the discharging of waste through the torpedo tubes. This was placed in weighted canvas torpedo sized bags to enable it to be blown out and to sink without trace.

We were in someone else's backyard which was constantly swept to clear away the trespassers they suspected would be lurking on their doorstep.

The taking of clandestine periscope photographs would need us to get up close and personal to the subject as it also would when recording the subject's noise signature. To hear and record radar transmissions our listening aerial had to be raised and exposed above the surface. If the objects of interest to us were shoreside it would mean us closing the coast where caution would be needed to avoid grounding, on the other hand recording sonar transmissions was freer of clutter when done in open waters the very waters that the soviet ships would be exercising using their search sonars. The information that we gathered would be disseminated by experts on our return.

This may all seem very exciting and nerve-wracking, which it would be at times, but we tended to live in two very different worlds as when off-watch and not sleeping, with ultra-quiet state being maintained throughout the boat, all our activities would need to be done quietly. A movie could not be shown therefore a favourite pastime was our cold war boredom buster 'Uckers'.

This helped keep our brains alert and stop our minds straying into the 'what if's' and the 'maybe's' of our other world. Uckers is a more complex and navalised version of the sedate board game Ludo. The rules of Uckers can vary ship to ship, but also to suit the local situation. The game would usually be played by two teams of two players but in situations such as ours when the normal duration of a watch would be three hours, unlike that of a surface ship which is four hours, to enable our contests to be played to completion we would use four players in each team. Two coming off watch could then take the place of those going on watch.

The game itself could be quite complicated, a game of strategy, especially when 'blobs' or 'mixi-blobs' were challenged or when being 'sucked back' from the home run pipe. It could be exciting and absorbing not only for the participants, but also for the spectators and supporters who would gather round the board. The games took on an even greater edge when fought out between us junior rates and either officers or senior rates.

I did witness one game which ended in severe acrimony luckily it was not during a mystery tour or long patrol. The game was between the petty officers mess team and that of the engine room articifers, the most mature crewmembers in age and experience of the whole crew. Before this long and hard fought contest was complete 'emergency stations' was sounded. This was a whole crew event which left the board unattended until 'emergency stations' were stood down. One of the returning P.O's accused the opposing side of having moved a counter – well so intense was this contest that the board ended up being thrown up in the air and the whole thing almost ended in fisticuffs – some example to us junior rates.

Russians are the acknowledged chess masters but I doubt they could master the passion and complexity of Uckers – perhaps that was why they came off second best in the cold war.

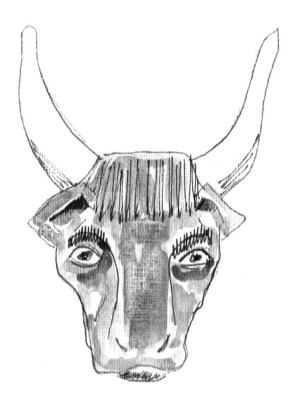

Bridging the gap

From spare crew I joined my first boat other than a 'T' class. She was the 'A' class Aurochs, I think the only one that hadn't been streamlined. She retained the 4" Qf gun mounted forward of the low bridge. It was more or less a 'pier head jump', just having time to pack some kit. I didn't know a soul on board but from the skipper an older, two and a half ringer (Lieutenant Commander) than I had been used to, downwards, they seemed a good bunch. The boat seemed more spacious and comfortable than the 'T' class. I liked the sewage tank W.C's which could be blown daily or when snorting, rather than the six position lever of the individual sanitary system I had been used to. With this system one had to ring the control room if dived, to ask "Permission to blow forward heads", unless snorting, then permission didn't have to be obtained. Sometimes the things would malfunction, causing a flashback and resulting in a crap spattered user. Bad enough to happen anywhere, but if you realize we had no showering or clothes washing facilities apart from a couple of hand basins, you can see it was very difficult to clean up afterward.

I can't remember much about the six weeks I spent on board except we hit a lot of rough weather to the north of Ireland where we were operating. Also I can't bring to mind any of the crew apart from the captain and the Jimmy.

I was impressed by the surface speed of the supercharged diesels, which gave us about 18 knots, this was about a three knot improvement over the 'T''s, far better when racing back to Gosport on the surface from 'Derry.

Back in spare crew a few weeks later, four or five of us herberts were shambling towards the jetties when a group of officers approached from the opposite direction. We took our right hands from out of our pockets to 'chop them off one' in our semblance of a salute. One of the officers called out to me by name. He was Lt. Champeney, first lieutenant of Aurochs. He came over, in front of my mates and shook me by the hand and thanked me. He said I had been a gust of good cheer for that six weeks and that he was sorry to lose me back to spare crew.

His words made me feel great, but I think they said more about him as an officer than about me just doing my job. Even in submarines there wasn't many in those days who would bridge the gap between 'us' and 'them' in that manner.

Perishers

The only time I served aboard a submarine which had been designed and built since the second world war was aboard the Porpoise. She was the lead boat of the eight of the class that were built. I served on her for less than six weeks, but not as a member of her crew as such. I don't say I was actually selected, more that I was shanghaied, the press gang still alive and well. The spirit of Andrew Miller, the most successful of press gang officers during the Napoleonic wars, he impressed so many that the Royal Navy was nicknamed The Andrew.

I had been working in the attack teacher at Fort Blockhouse, HMS Dolphin. This was the forerunner of the modern simulator. On its lower deck (floor) was a mock up of a submarine's control room – complete with periscopes, TCSS (fruit machine), ARL table which was linked to gyro compass and the ships log (I'm not sure how this was all achieved mechanically in this mock up situation, but it all seemed realistic). I was there to operate the time/bearing or back plot as we called it. I would be plotting the sonar bearings I received through my headphones. Any writing I did with my chinagraph pencil on the back of the vertically mounted clear perspex plot, had to be done back to front so those studying the plot from the front could make sense of it. (I was what you might call a backward writer).

At other times I would maintain the charts pinned over the ARL table, which tracked the movements of the submarine since a given position (this could be the diving position or start of the attack position). A light linked to the gyro compass and ships log, shone up from below, through the glass top of the table and was visible through the paper of the chart where its progress could be traced with pencil. The target and escorts tracks would be plotted on the chart as of course would any visual or other fixes we managed to obtain, thus we had a reasonable picture of the tactical situation.

The top deck of the attack teacher represented the surface of the sea upon which the teacher (training commander) had hundreds of exact replicas in miniature of naval and merchant ships of many nationalities to deploy, either as single targets or as escorted convoys. Viewed through the periscope it looked very realistic as these targets could be made to behave as any real ship or formation in a war zone would. I was not conversant with the finer points of how this whole set-up worked, only from the point of view of the user. The attack teacher was staffed by members of the W.R.N.S. (Wrens to us) and they really knew their stuff.

Anyway, how I got from there to the Porpoise as part of the team headed by teacher – the redoubtable Commander Wemyss – I don't know. Before I had time to ponder that question we were heading north to Rothsay, Isle of Bute, to rendezvous with the Perishers, as the prospective submarine commanders were called. The adjacent exercise areas would be the arena where the Perishers skill and experience would be tested. It was make or break, any or even all could pass or fail. Failure would be the end of the candidate's career in submarines. I think there were five of them on this course. All of them were experienced First

Lieutenants who had been recommended and selected for the course and even though their own C.O's would have allowed them to make some dummy attacks nothing they had done to date would compare to the pressure cooker atmosphere of the Perisher.

Over the years, since leaving the service, I have watched two different series on TV. Both gave a good insight of the Perisher course. One course was held aboard an Oreron class boat (quite similar to the Porpoise) the other was held aboard a nuclear attack boat of the new 'T' class. The scope of both series did not extend downward to explore how these pressures affected the submarine's crew, especially those in the attack team. They who had to support 'him at the periscope' to get him where he wanted to be and at the right time to make the attack and to deal with the aftermath.

The Porpoise's own C.O, a senior Lieutenant Commander, destined for greater things in the service, had to leave 'his' submarine in the equally capable hands of the teacher, who in turn had to allow whichever of the Perishers was conducting the attack a certain amount of latitude in his temporary command, but be ready to step in and take over in time, should a potentially dangerous situation occur. There were tensions between all these leading actors in the drama, but also for the Porpoise's own First Lieutenant, trying to maintain trim and the two planesmen keeping the boat level and at a precise periscope depth to avoid ducking the 'scope under the surface, especially at a critical time during the attack, or exposing too much of the 'scope, making it an easily identifiable visual or radar contact.

The sonarmen were under pressure to discern and disseminate what their ears were telling them, likewise, I felt under pressure behind the time bearing plot trying to produce a curve from the sonar reports to assist in making a prediction of where the target was likely to be to enable the Perisher to get in an attacking position.

He would be consulting the ARL plot and the fruit machine, taking fleeting periscope bearings and angle on the bow of the target. Periscope up again for quick all round sweep, checking the zig-zag courses of the escorts and making sure none were homing in for an attack on us. He may decide to go deep and run in to clear one of the outer escort screen, continually checking his stopwatch, making mental calculations before deciding when it should be safe to return to periscope depth again. The sonar 'audible picture' could be confusing with so much H.E. (hydrophone effect) making it impossible to pick out individual ships propellers. My heart was always in my mouth when we came up 'blind' and I don't suppose I was the only one, although all tried to appear unconcerned, as the periscope rose to enable, the all important, first quick all round sweep. If the handles were snapped up immediately (signifying down periscope) and simultaneously the curt order "Flood Q 120ft" was given we knew things were not rosy.

Hopefully though, we would have got inside the outer escort and be in the attacking position we all desired. None of us wanted to be a cause for the Perisher not to shine or to break off the attack prematurely and miss 'sinking' the target. This after all was our raison d'etre. Me thinks me enjoyed it more, all these years later as an armchair pundit watching it on TV than I did at the time peering through the TB plot watching the opera unfold inside a cauldron.

Four of the five Perishers made the grade required by teacher and went on to become submarine commanders. There were no failures as such, the fifth member of the course would return to general service. They would gain a very high grade officer.

With regard to the Porpoise, she was an unknown fish to me and I felt like a fish out of water – lost. Everything about her was strange – the fore-ends or torpedo handling space as I think they called it, seemed immense and cathedral like. I was allocated a bunk somewhere near the forrard mess in a little cranny, it took me a few goes to find it in the dimmed lighting. I actually slept through harbour stations on one occasion and awoke to find we were at sea. Nobody even missed my absence.

You couldn't go from a 'T' or 'A' class without doing some familiarization course first as everything was different – the valves and controls and most of the machinery , I remember one evening going with a P.O. to operate the gash ejector, a new experience for me. It seemed a complex operation just to get rid of waste food, etc. Different to the torpedo sized, weighted canvas bags we used to discharge our waste through the torpedo tubes on a 'T' boat.

I suppose all things considered you could say I had been taken out of my comfort zone to which I would be quite happy to return.

Red dog, The pirates Kai Jars
and a slow commotion.

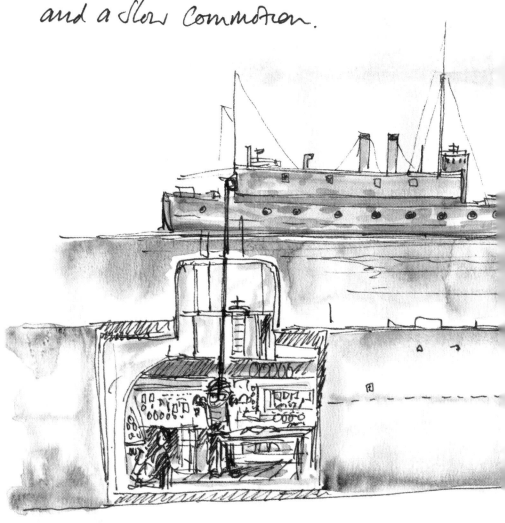

Red dog, The pirates Kai Jars and a Slow Commotion.

It had been a long, hot slog across the Indian Ocean since leaving Colombo. This was new territory for me, as the Superb had never gone very far east of Ceylon. I thought it hot then, but even more so now – we had no scuttles to open or wind scoops to put out. There not being much room on the bridge for more than two or three extra persons to enjoy the sun's rays, so there was always a gathering in the Control Room, at the foot of the ladder, where there was at least some air movement, albeit hot rushing air being sucked in by the main engines.

Most of us from the forrard mess would rarely go aft, so didn't pay much attention to what went on back there. We thought it hot forrard, but the engineers had it worse and noisy, so on those rare occasions we didn't linger too long, as it was only a narrow passageway between the two engines and one had to dodge one of the stokers busy with his lubricating can or whatever they did, as they fussed over their noisy chargers. It was only if one of them threw a shoe or whatever else thoroughbreds or carthorses do, that we became concerned, especially if we were at our racing speed of 14 knots to get in early enough for a run ashore.

I had been on one boat where the Jimmy would adjust our trim, to further bury the screws and lift the bow. He swore it gave us an extra quarter of a knot – much more speed and we would be planing! Anyway, on this voyage we had no such problem, in fact we must have been ahead of our schedule to enter the Malacca Straits, as the skipper decided we would dive and carry out a few evolutions and emergency drills. Hydroplanes and steering in emergency, using the hand pumps, that sort of thing, anything to raise a sweat!

As the Navy and NATO needed to know where its own submarines were at all times, whenever we were en route, either on the surface or snorting, we would operate within a 'moving box' which enabled the captain some freedom of manoeuvre, while also enabling base operations staff to keep tabs on us. There were strict procedures to be followed concerning 'diving' and 'surfacing' signals as non-compliance would result in a 'submiss' or 'subsunk' being instituted, which would involve a massive search and rescue effort.

While dived he wanted to carry out an attack, well a mock one anyway, on one of the many ships that would be heading toward the Straits. I haven't mentioned too much about the sonar operators, if we of the radar department were the long range eyes, they were the long range ears and the most important source of information the Captain had at his disposal. I'm not sure who coined the term slow-commotion, it was either the Captain or the HSD (meaning higher sonar detector, an old name for the senior sonar operator) but anway the search narrowed down to one particular ship headed our way. As normal, sonar had been asked to classify the hydrophone effect of this slow approaching ship and the best that was offered was that it was a slow-commotion, partly because of her lack of speed, but also because of the clanging and banging of her engines. When it came into periscope view, it was described as looking like one of the old river gunboats, with a low freeboard, rusty and neglected. Wouldn't have been worth a torpedo, we went deep and let her pass, she would have shaken to bits with fright if our periscope was sighted. Thereafter, other ships of that ilk were classified by that term.

After surfacing it was decided that we would carry out another attack, but this time it would be using our Lanchester sub machine guns, our personal weapons, against a couple of paint drums the scratcher would toss overboard, an unequal contest. We would be vigilant for pirates and gun runners throughout the five hundred mile run down the Straits, I'm not sure what we would look out for as Sumatran pirates don't wear peg legs or parrots.

The Lanchesters were normally kept chained into glass-fronted cabinets outside of our mess and we didn't often get the chance for target practice. It fired a 9mm parabellum round, at 600 rounds per minute. The magazine box was loaded with 50 rounds. We would each carry three of these magazines in a pouch if we were on a boarding party. It was just a matter of slamming the box into the housing on the left side of the weapon, the spent cartridges ejected on the right. We could fix a long bladed bayonet to it, making it a good close-quarter weapon. It was much better than the Sten gun that the army used, sturdier, as it had the same wooden stock as the Lee Enfield rifles we had trained with at Browndown Ranges. Also the stock had the storage for the oiler and pull through, which we would use at the end of the shoot. The atmosphere within the boat was often moisture laden, not good for a gun's working parts.

The paint drums didn't stand a chance and we claimed two kills.

We did investigate a couple of junks fairly close inshore one time, but once alongside we saw they housed families, a few kids and a couple of chickens, some sacks of rice, but no pirates.

It is said that a quarter of the world's traded goods pass through the

Malacca Straits, even though it is not deep enough to accommodate the largest ships and the laden super tankers which have to transit the Lombok Straits, or another of the deep water channels. As you near Singapore the Phillips Channel is only a mile and a half wide, making it one of the busiest of the choke points.

On my second day in Singapore, I went with one of our sparkers up to the Royal Navy Wireless Station at Kranji, an hour and a half or so by Navy transport, it was a forest of aerials in the jungle. We went to visit his mate, an ex-submariner sparker, who I knew from Dolphin. We would spend a few days there as it was also used as a rest camp, having a good outside pool, cinema and bowling alley – plus a few wrens. From here we could explore some of the surrounding jungle.

On returning to the dockyard and the boat, the tanky told us how he and the chef had teamed up with some American submariners, one of whom was their chef, a real character known as Red Dog, probably on account of his red hair and hound dog look. They had all ended up at a honky tonk joint on the infamous Bugis Street, where the 'girls' there made a real fuss of them, fawning around them and sitting on their laps. Our lads knew these were kai tais - transgender boy/girls. Not so Red Dog, he was in love with one of these flamboyantly dressed kai tais. Try as they might neither Red Dog's crew mates, nor our lads, could tear him away from his new love, so in the end they left him there. The Americans had been invited down our boat at 'up spirits' for rum and some beer, which we had by the crate, their boats being dry. It seems Red Dog had a very rude awakening next to his boy/girl and was now a laughing stock, his face as red as his hair. He was staying on board until they sailed.

I shifted my kit ashore to HMS Terror, the shore base, to await transport to Hong Kong being supernumerary, as there were five radar plot ratings on board, there should only be three for watch keeping and the fourth was tanky on day work.

Curses and Misadventures

Moving ashore with me to HMS Terror the shore establishment at Sembewang, Singapore, was another able seaman who I knew as 'Enry, short for Henry, but that wasn't his name. It was because laying down he was about 6ft 2ins, a long fellow[1]. He wasn't a poet he was a fore-endsman, underwater weapons, in other words a torpedoman. Standing up I think he was about 6ft 12ins, a giant amongst us lowly souls, although strangely enough there seemed to be a lot of big fellows in submarines. 'Enry told me he was quite happy to put up with the cramped conditions to get away from general service with its kit musters, parades and pettifogging dress codes. A bit like myself, though I didn't bang my head as often as he did. He got his nicknames 'Longfellow' and 'Higher Waffer' when serving on the 'Totem'.

The boat had been presented with a totem pole by the Cowichan, a Canadian Red Indian tribe. I had seen the totem pole at various times over the years, as when in harbour the pole would stand in front of the Totem's fin. 'Enry told me that they treated the pole with reverence, through fear of invoking the curse that the tribesmen had protected it with. During a visit to Nova Scotia some years later the pole was stolen or spirited away. If stolen the thieves will have suffered an untimely end.... scalped no doubt. The Totem was sold to the Israeli Navy in 1968 and renamed 'Dakar'. Unfortunately it did not lift the curse, as she was lost with her whole crew on the delivery voyage somewhere south east of Cyprus.

'Enry amused me when he said that the main reasons that he preferred to be the fore-endsman of the watch was firstly because he was a rubbish fore-planesman, secondly, he liked to fall out of his pit into the 'office' as it cut out the travelling time. No ducking down the alley for our long tall sally. His kitbag, suitcase and remainder of his kit had been shipped out from the UK and were awaiting him at HMS Terror. He was en route to the 4th Submarine Squadron, based at HMAS Penguin, Syd-

---

[1]American poet, Henry Wadsworth Longfellow 1807-1882 wrote Hiawatha.

ney, Australia. He would be joining one of the boats soon to be calling at Singapore on their way to Aussie, either the 'Trump', 'Taciturn' or 'Tabard'. If it was Tabard he joined, I hope he ducked when the Aussie frigate 'Queenborough' sliced through her fin while she was dived, 8 May 1963. Luckily no injuries to either crew, just another own goal by a friendly.

A 'T' conversion, the 'Turpin' which I had been aboard as a boy at Chatham Navy Days and was named after Dick Turpin the infamous highwayman who frequented Runwell Hill, robbing travelers (which is close to where I live but long before I was born) – well she was also sold to the Israelis and renamed 'Leviathan' in 1967. Although she wasn't under any curse to my knowledge, two of her crew were washed off of her casing and drowned. Her first Israeli Commander, his wife, son and a grandson, were murdered by a Palestinian terrorist while at a restaurant in Haifa, Israel, 4 October 2003. During Turpin's earlier life in the Royal Navy, she suffered bad cracking to both of her main engines while in the West Indies. The Navy sent a Bustler class convoy escort tug, the 'Samsonia' to tow her the 5,000 miles back to the UK. This class of tug were designed to be able to accommodate up to 200 crewmen of stricken ships and had a large frozen food capacity to be able to feed those taken on board. It took 28 days to tow Turpin home – the slowest highwayman on record.

In 1968 another 'T' conversion, the 'Truncheon' was transferred to Israel. She was renamed 'Dolphin', the only time I went aboard her was in Guzz (Navy term for Devonport). I was there on my last boat the 'Talent', she having just completed refit in Devonport dockyard. I went aboard Truncheon to see my old shipmate, Ray 'Badges' Duckett, one of her stokers. Badges, his lovely wife Shirley and two small children had been at our wedding in Malta along with most of Tiptoe's crew. I thought this was a good reason to share his rum issue and that of some of his hospitable messmates.

On leaving the boat I was negotiating the passageway and about to step over the coaming of the accommodation space watertight door into the fore-ends, when I had to step aside, as one does, to make way for her Captain, who had just come aboard. I immediately recognized the smart 'two and a half ringer', a Nelson-like figure, but with both arms and eyes. Seeing me he stopped almost aghast and asked me what I was doing aboard his submarine. I think he was relieved when I said I was just visiting one of his stalwarts. We had history, as my Jimmy, his eloquence had helped get me out of a very tight spot in Gibraltar some five years earlier and I thank him for that. The story will remain untold, too many machinations to mention, as it says in the song, well almost.

The Seventh Submarine Squadron

I thought it strange that 'T' conversions were being sent to operate from the Australian base, as the Pacific was what the 'A' class had been designed for with their range, surface speed and air conditioning. After giving it some thought I realized that part of the conversion for the 'T''s was using the gun tower as a cab style bridge, fitting any sort of gun, even a low calibre one would mean its crew would have to man it by climbing down from the bridge – hardly satisfactory. 'A' class boats were also serving out in Canada, so the number of boats available was limited. Those boats of the seventh squadron based in Singapore had all been streamlined, although some still had the folding snort mast, well the 'Andrew' and 'Alliance' had, because I had seen theirs in the down position on the port after casing. The 'Anchorite', 'Auriga' and 'Ambush' were the other boats. All of the boats had the large bulbous sonar dome fitted right forrard. Being an ex-buoy jumper myself I could tell it must have made it difficult when picking up a buoy. Most, if not all, had been fitted with a deck gun for use in anti-piracy, gun running, etc, during the Indonesian campaign. The gun was either the 4" or a 20mm, it had a band-stand style guardrail surrounding it, to protect its crew from being washed or knocked overboard. The Alliance was sporting camouflage paintwork for work close inshore – the only time I've seen an R.N. submarine in anything other than Henry Ford's shiny black. Having this arrangement of deck gun it would be impossible to carry out the traditional gun action I described earlier, as the boat would have to surface properly before allowing the gun crew to clamber out of the gun tower hatch and climb down to the fore casing. A case of needs must, it being difficult, expensive and overkill to sink a junk drawing two feet of water with a fan of torpedoes.

Galley Slaves

The Coxswain, the senior seaman and normally a chief petty officer, has many responsibilities including ordering and maintaining food supplies and planning menus along with the chef and his own right hand man, the tanky.

The chef's kingdom is an electric powered galley measuring about six foot by four foot. He produces a cooked breakfast and a two or three course dinner daily for the crew of fifty five to sixty fit young men. Mealtimes were a highlight whether days were hectic or humdrum. The other, brighter highlight, being 'up spirits'. This was done half an hour before dinner, usually 11.30 a.m.

He cooked these meals whenever we were away from a base or depot ship. Sometimes he also made bread and at other times he baked rolls. Many times over the years since leaving the Andrew I hear people, working in pubs or restaurants, saying "Mustn't upset the chef, he's under pressure". It takes a special type to contend with what submarine life threw up. The boat on the surface, or even sometimes at periscope depth, could be pitching, rolling or corkscrewing. Anyone working or moving about would be clinging on for dear life.

Only once did I see a chef lose his equilibrium. At the behest of the cox'n he was baking a couple of hundred rolls, which the Jimmy was aware of, and about half way through this we came up periscope depth and commenced snorting. Snorting in rough weather, and/or the boat out of trim caused pressure to fluctuate – not good for the eardrums and also not good when expecting dough to rise.

I was on the foreplanes, struggling to keep the depth at forty five feet (the depth required to keep the periscope lens and the snort head just above the surface). Most of the time I was 'chasing the bubble'. You will have to get a submariner to explain that, it would take me a whole page and bore you stupid in the process. It was then that I heard a metallic clatter, as a galley tray came skidding over the control room decking and a cascade of half risen bread rolls came to rest in the bilges, on the chart table and down the periscope wells. I turned my head to see the back of the angry chef as he stormed forrard. Nobody said a word, the officer of the watch, the torpedo officer, normally a tyrant, seemed unusually intent at the periscope. After a few minutes he turned and said "Get tanky to come and clear them up" and went back to his periscope. We didn't get the nice fresh rolls we were looking forward to!

We soon settled back to routine, the chef did no more baking, just producing his gourmet pot mess and other speciality dishes, including my favourite 'babies heads' and on Sundays the traditional roast.

As all good things do eventually, our Western Atlantic foray came to an end, without any success, as being the boat captained by the most junior of C.O.'s we had been positioned in the most far flung of areas. Our furthest point westwards was out toward Newfoundland, the area having the worst weather. Likely targets would have been hopelessly lost if they came into view of our periscopes so there was little hope of any glory for our skipper.

The trip ended with a few days visit to the city port of Lorient on France's west coast. We berthed within the massive former U-boat pens, built to accommodate thirty of Germany's wartime submarines on a fifty acre site. The bunkers had three metre thick reinforced concrete roofs, floating armoured doors protected their entrance. This was now the base for some of France's diesel submarines. Moored inside were three of their Daphne class boats. As France had to start from scratch after the war, these boats were modern. They were smaller than us, a 'T' class, but deeper diving, quiet and manoeuvrable with a small number of crew. The French were very hospitable and we drank some fine wines down in their mess. It's funny, as a nation we tend to denigrate the French, but I was impressed with their boats and also by the efficiency of their submariners.

Anyway, the main aim of all this waffle is to get to the point that our Captain and officers had arranged us to put on a 'sods opera' to be held in the French Navy's canteen. We were all expected to make a contribution to the evening entertainment. I teamed up with one of the engine room tiffies and the bunting tosser. Both had good voices which would mask my tuneless contribution. From our French friends we borrowed three sailors' hats, the ones with the red bobble on top. I chose for us to sing our version of the recent release by Edith Piaf of 'Non, Je ne

216

regrette rien', changing the words to:-

> Non, non baguettes
>
> Non, monsieur le chef
>
> Let there be no baguettes
>
> Non je ne regrette rien

We would make our entrance, galley trays held high, doing a high kicking can-can. At the end of the routine we tipped the galley trays full of stale rolls over the Jimmy's table to the amusement of all, particularly the chef. The First Lieutenant's French officer guests seemed bemused by it all.

We had no potato peeling machine in those days. Instead, each mess had to provide the chef with the amount they needed. Once back in the UK on a fine day, and if we were at some isolated mooring and out of sight of the grey funnel line, we would sit up on the casing round by the forrard escape hatch to peel the spuds. Our equivalent of office workers gathering round the drinks machine except we had no drinks, only spuds.

There would be a few of us from the forward mess, mainly seamen, the tanky who was also the P.O.'s messman, a stoker - the messman for the tiffys, the steward who looked after the Captain and the wardroom and some stokers from the after mess. It was rare to see stokers from back aft. While our duties at sea rarely took us aft of the control room, theirs even more rarely brought them forward of the control room, the only exception being the outside wrecker, as we called the leading stoker who maintained equipment outside of the engine room. It was also a very rare occasion for oilies to come up on the bridge for fresh air if we were on the surface at sea unless there was something to see apart from the sea. Fresh air, I think, was anathema to most of them.

So it was good to sit around, peel spuds and spin a few yarns. Sometimes it was just "Do you know old so and so on the Trump", or "Our Jimmy on the Tally-Ho who always ate tins of snails when officer of the watch", or "When I was on Artful", or about the notorious wardroom steward by the name of 'Buckwheat' Harris, upset about something, taped a kipper to the underside of the wardroom table before going on leave. About ten days into his leave he got a telegram from the Jimmy "We know what it is, but where is it?".

This particular day Abe Lincoln, a stoker whose face looked like a box of spanners, happened to mention a Chinese girl he had met in Hong Kong. 'Who was she, no nose Nelly' taunted one of his fellow stokers. They all laughed at Abe, they thought he was spinning them a line. Abe turned to me and said "Tell them about Lin Ling". "O.k." I said, "I've never mentioned it to anyone before".

The Story of Lin Ling

I had arrived in Hong Kong from Singapore, having taken passage through the South China Sea aboard an RFA supply ship. I reported to the regulating office, they told me the 'A' class boat I was expecting to join was in dock in Sidney, Australia and was not due to return for about six weeks. They told me that a stoker called Lincoln was also waiting to rejoin her after being discharged from the military hospital, his jaw had been broken during a fracas in the China Fleet Club. He was now living ashore in a flat in Kowloon. The regulating office didn't know what to do with me and when I asked if I could work alongside Abe in the dockyard they readily agreed. Abe was supposedly responsible for maintaining some emergency generators and donkey boilers on the jetties. We spent a lot of time fishing off the jetty – well we had a line with a hook on it but I don't remember catching anything!

It was here that we met Jenny, a Chinese woman who supplied side parties to paint and clean rust from visiting warships. We didn't know it at the time but she was well known and respected by the Navy. As she sat with us she reeled off a list of admirals, ships captains and others she knew. She told us she also knew Lord and Lady Mountbatten. When she learned that Abe was living in a flat in Kowloon she said she knew a girl who would do his washing and cleaning.

That evening Abe and I caught the Star Ferry to Kowloon, Jenny was going to meet us at the ferry terminal. We waited for some while and were about to give up and go to Abe's local bar the Won Son when Jenny showed up. With her was the loveliest Chinese girl I'd ever seen, small and delicate with beautiful almond shaped eyes and long black hair. The four of us went to Abe's penthouse where I had been kipping in the living area. Abe was a wizard on the six valve chest and with an oily bilge pump but his domestic skills were lacking – the place was a doss hole.

Lin Ling took over and we did what we did best, spending a couple of hours in the Won Son bar after our token appearance at the dockyard. Abe always made a point of ringing the engineers' office with a list of faults he had corrected or was going to correct. After a while they more or less said don't keep bothering them with phone calls, just do what needs to be done. As we only had the uniforms we had carried with us we started to wear khaki shirts and shorts. We didn't look Navy and were ignored by any officers or senior rates that passed by. We disappeared under the radar.

Gradually Abe's flat became sparkling. Lin Ling always had a tray of food waiting for us – my first real introduction to Chinese food. Abe treated her well and used to buy her little things. When she went to visit her mother, Abe and I sent presents – usually cigarettes. She worshipped Abe. Most days she went off to a class where she was studying English. I used to help her pronounce the words she had learned and helped her put them into sentences.

One day she turned up carrying what we called a 'donkey's breakfast'. This was a small rolled up mattress stuffed with reeds or straw. She decided to move in and slept on the floor of Abe's room – it was easier for her as we no longer felt we needed to go to the dockyard and were coming in later and later from the Won Son. The regulating office had put us on ration allowance. It was easier for them than getting us victualed into a mess somewhere and issuing us with some kit. They knew where to find us if we were wanted. They had their hands full as the harbour was bursting with ships, usually one of our aircraft or commando carriers, a host of destroyers and frigates, as well as U.S. ships visiting for R & R, the Vietnam war was in full swing.

On one of our visits to the dockyard the engineers' office messenger came to summon Abe to the office. Abe panicked, he put some old overalls over his shirt and shorts, tucked an oily rag into his top pocket and rubbed some grease into his hands, which he was cleaning off with cotton waste as he entered the office. The chief stoker rose from behind a mountain of paperwork on his desk. "Lincoln, sorry you've had to cope alone" he said "we've got to send someone from our staff to the fleet ball. Take these tickets for you and your oppo and you can each take a guest, it'll be a free evening for you". Abe was more than relieved. I had no one to take but we decided to go with Lin Ling.

She was reluctant to go but we took her down to the little tailor's shop which we passed each day on the way to the ferry. We often had a little joke with the old mandarin who was usually seated in a battered armchair outside his shop. He showed us his book of designs and Abe picked out a clinging gown in a dark green silk with a flower pattern on the bodice. Lin Ling was measured up and within two days the gown and a matching clutch bag were ready.

The shoemaker a couple of doors away had made some high heeled slippers for her tiny feet. As we had no tropical uniforms the tailor made us each a pair of dark blue trousers with a black stripe sewn down the outside seam. We chose a white jacket each from his rail and with some soft calf leather boots from the shoemaker's we looked as if we were members of some regimental club or colonial clan.

The three of us went to the same barber's shop and whilst Abe and I were being shaved and shorn, Lin Ling was being fussed over by three girl hairdressers. They were all giggling – it was the first time either of us had heard Lin Ling let herself go.

The evening of the ball we had arranged a cab to pick us up at the Won Son. We looked the smartest we'd ever been. Lin Ling looked stunning as if she'd stepped out of a fashion magazine. As she stepped daintily from the cab all eyes were on her.

The doorman walked forward to assist her up the steps, she smiled at him and plucked a flower from the small posy she carried and pressed it into his hand. She smiled radiantly at the senior bemedalled officers and their ladies and lowered her gaze from the admiring glances of the younger and the not so young uniformed men. Her eyes were shining as she sipped a cocktail from a long stemmed glass. It was a real glittering occasion and to outsiders it must have seemed she was brought up to this. She was too shy and unsure of her English to get into any deep conversation with anyone who tried, but she had a word for them all.

As we sat at the table Abe and I felt out of our depth. Only ever having been used to a knife, fork and spoon, we now had a whole array of them as well as three different glasses to choose from. It didn't matter, nobody paid any attention to us, Lin Ling was the centre of attention. Chopsticks had been provided for the many Chinese dignitaries around the long tables. Lin Ling was having fun teaching a medical commander and his wife to use them.

After the port was passed, the Queen toasted and the speeches delivered, it was time for the army dance band to strike up. Soon, a succession of handsome hopefuls tried to entice Lin Ling to dance. She refused them all except when Abe asked her – she almost leapt into his arms. With any stretch of a vivid imagination you could not describe Abe as handsome but as they danced I could see something about him. His face had the soulful look of a basset hound. (He used to embarrass me by saying he wished he looked like me – but I didn't say that in my story.)

I paused what I was saying, stood up and walked over to the gangway and looked down into the water swirling through the concrete pillars of the jetty. "God, Abe must be rigged like a donkey" said one of the stokers. With that the tanky, a three badged killik sonarman rounded on the stoker "Shut up you turd" he snapped, then he said to me "What happened". He sensed I had a reason for stopping. I glanced at Abe who had a far away look on his face, the pain was etched on his rugged features. He looked at me and nodded.

I said it had been a magical evening which finished late. The beers, the wine and the port had taken their effect. It was late when we awoke.

Lin Ling was gone. She often visited a relative in the New Territories before going to her classes. "Jeez, I've got a mouth like the inside of a rickshaw boy's jockstrap" said Abe. "Mine's like the bottom of a parrot's cage" I said, "All shit and sandpaper". There was a banging from the door below which led to the street. Bleary eyed we looked down to the street below. There stood a naval patrolman. I called out of the window to him. He shouted back "Chop chop, pack your gear and get in the van, you're joining a submarine that's on her way back to Singers. They've landed four of their crew with typhoid or something." We just had time to write a note to Lin Ling. We left with it all the Hong Kong dollars we had. We didn't know what else we could do, and that was that. I don't think Abe spoke to anyone for a week.

"More like Coney Island" sez I

Arriving back at Dolphin from the far flung there had been quite a few changes during our absence. New accommodation blocks had been completed, one each for chiefs and P.O.'s and a couple for junior rates.

The choofs and poofs (as junior rates jokingly called them) had single cabins and waiter service dining hall. Each mess had a bar which was better stocked than the 'Bricklayers Arms'. The car parks outside were bursting at the seams – easy credit had arrived. "It's more like Manhattan Island these days" retorted Pusser Hill. "More like Coney Island" sez I, "all we need is a fun fair and candy floss and you'll never get them back to sea".

I never was accommodated in the new junior rates blocks. They had small four man dorms. Our crew were in the original dorms, close to the Dining Hall, which could sleep all of our junior rates, much better for banter and for winding each other up.

The standard of the food was now as good as I've had anywhere, plentiful and on a self service basis. Sometimes I'd have beef chow mein plus a ladle of Lancashire hot-pot, just because it was there. Luckily they hadn't done away with 'babies heads'.

A new arrival at Dolphin was Doctor No, the new medical commander. He had been sent by God to counter the new wave gluttony. His upper floor office at the medical centre overlooked the main thoroughfare. He spent his day bird watching to spot the plump turkeys and overfed peasants. The overweights would try all sorts to avoid his diet enforcing attention. Luckily I could eat what I liked, as long as I kept my liquid intake up to balance it, I never put on the poundage.

Whilst in Dolphin I had to refresh my SETT (escape training). I had to slot in with a batch of trainee submariners. Not the same as going through with one's own crew mates, whose banter helped ease the tensions – especially when doing the two man escape, when one had to rely on the other bloke playing his part.

MALTESE=FALCON

Maltese Falcons and
a Greek Odyssey

My posting to Malta as 'spare crew' aboard the depot ship 'Ausonia'
conjured pictures in my mind of lazing in the sun on golden beaches and
swimming in crystal clear water. After touching down at Luqa the Cu-
nard Eagle DC6 taxied to the small terminal. Peering out of its side windows I thought how dry and dusty everything looked. The half dozen
of us submariners on board were met by an R.N. truck and its Maltese
driver to be taken to the submarine base at Manoel Island which is in
Lazeretto Creek.

As a schoolboy I was not particularly imaginative nor was I an avid student of history. I noticed that certain historical events captured the attention of many of the boys. One of these was the crusades to defend the Holy Lands from Islam. The Knights of Malta, who had become a military order, were rewarded by Charles V of Spain for their part in the crusades by the gift of Malta, Gozo and Tripoli, in exchange for an annual fee of one Maltese falcon. Under their grand master Jean de le Valette (after whom the capital Valetta, or Valletta as it is also called, was named). The 700 Knights of different nationalities and their soldiers about 8,000 strong withstood the siege by the ottomans in 1565 under Suleiman the Magnificent, Sultan of Turkey. Little did I know that within a few months of my arrival in Malta, I would be living for a while in Fort St Angelo, one of the bastions of this defence. As well as reading Biggles I had also read much about the Second World War, the war in the Mediterranean and in particular the siege of Malta by the air forces of the axis partners, Germany and Italy.

Looking at the buildings as we drove through the built up areas on our way to Sliema and our base at Lazeretto Creek I could see no evidence of the huge tonnage of high explosive bombs that had been dropped. During March and April of 1942 alone, this was more than that dropped on London during the blitz and I knew how much devastation that had caused. I also knew that the base to which we were headed had been one of the prime targets as the Royal Navy's submarines based there were causing havoc to the supply lines of the axis armies in Libya, which were aiming to advance into Egypt and across Africa.

King George VI visited Malta and on the 15th April 1942 awarded the George Cross, the highest award for civilian valour, to the island and people of Malta. Malta dockyard was converted to civilian use in 1959, the Tiptoe which I joined toward the end of her re-fit, must have been amongst the last of Royal Navy ships to have been re-fitted there.

Our Maltese driver brought the R.N. truck to a halt alongside the depot ship Ausonia. When I carried my kit bag up to her upper deck I could see four of the service's eight 'T' conversion boats at her trots. I was to find that this was a very rare occasion to have four alongside at any one time.

These boats were ones built around 1944 and, unlike those 'T' class built earlier, were of all welded hull construction. The conversion involved cutting the hull and inserting another section, allowing the larger battery required to enable higher underwater speeds. This was aided by fitting a streamlined fin to enclose the periscopes, the latest periscopic snort mast, as well as the aerial mast for the much improved radar set. The gun was removed and in its place a low cab-style bridge was fitted forward of the fin. Aluminium was used in place of steel to construct the casing. Taking all into consideration these boats were to prove an efficient stop gap until the Porpoise class and the later Oberon's were all in commission – well that's the opinion of an ordinary dab-toe.

I had hardly stowed my kit aboard Ausonia when the drafting cox-swain said I was needed aboard 'Thermopylae' as she was shorthanded and about to sail. These last minute postings we knew as 'pier-head jumps'. The general service crew of Ausonia and most of the submarine crews, as well as the spare crew, were on married accompanied postings. They lived ashore in married quarters when not at sea or harbour duty. It created less upheaval to send the single men on these pier-head jumps. Thus on this, and a number of other occasions, I went to cover someone of a specialization other than my own radar plot.

Thermop was on her way to Piraeus, Greece. She had the feel of a happy boat and I soon fitted in. The Captain obviously enjoyed a swim and as we were transiting on the surface, when the opportunity arose and sea conditions allowed, he would stop the submarine, pipe "Hands to bathe" over the tannoy system and be amongst the first to dive in.

Piraeus is the sea port of Athens where I did the usual tourist trail. However, far more memorable to me was the visit a large contingent of us made to the village after which we were named. We stood on the mountain pass where Leonidas and his 300 Spartans, in 480 BC, defend-ed against and defeated the invading Persians and then about 200 years later the Greeks held the Gauls for several months before ultimately being defeated.

We dined al fresco with the villagers and drank their wines. We had brought with us crates of beer and plenty of cigarettes for them. We played their football team and lost and our tug of war team beat theirs. Towards the end of our stay at Piraeus the electrical officer asked three of us if we wished to hike back across country and rejoin the boat at the far end of the Corinth canal. I remember the rugged terrain and the scorching heat, also I recall climbing a high hill which had a monastery at its summit. The flagons of wine, the bread and goats cheese the monks served us was probably the best snack I've ever had – maybe because we were parched and ravenous.

After rejoining the boat she turned her bow towards Malta where we were to make ready for a forthcoming exercise against units of the US 6th Fleet.

Tread Softly Carry a big Stick

With this in mind you could think this a good motto for a submarine named Tiptoe. She could tread softly, with a well trained crew keeping noise to a minimum and who would ensure everything under the casing was secure and the flaps tightened down. Being a 'T' conversion she had been cut in half and had another section welded in allowing for more battery power, plus another pair of main motors, hence greater underwater speed, like converting the family Ford into a Ferrari. She also had a streamlined fin, smoothing out the water flowing around the periscopes, snort mast and aerials. Forward of the fin the gun had been removed and in its place was now a low, cab style bridge. No longer was there a jumping wire with the main, low and high frequency wireless aerials attached. They were now housed inside the fin. The higher underwater speed allowed these converted boats better opportunity to track and attack surface and submarine targets and if necessary to make good their escape.

All machines were resilient mounted to prevent noise being transmitted though the hull, the pipe work and cables leading to them designed to allow movement, preventing vibration. Tiptoe was fitted with reduced noise propellers which would be inspected for any damage to the blades before going on patrol. Even small chips to the metal on the blade could cause cavitation noise.

The big stick was the six 21 inch (diameter) torpedoes in the bow tubes, as well as the reloads stowed in the fore-ends.

Tiptoe's official crest shows a ballerina wearing a white dress dancing in front of a blue background. A prized possession in her wardroom was one of ballerina Margot Fontaine's ballet shoes, kept in a glass case.

Before her conversion Tiptoe had starred in the film 'We dive at dawn' co-starring John Mills. Submarine warfare requirements have moved on since those days, now on a war patrol, or cold war mission, it would be prudent to submerge once in water deep enough and stay dived, snorting as required to charge batteries, for the length of the patrol which could be up to five or six weeks.

I spent some time on Tiptoe, at sea, which included visits to a number of Mediterranean ports, one of which must have been Izmir, Turkey, as I have a photograph of us alongside the jetty there. I was on loan from spare crew, but left her when she went for refit in Malta dockyard.

Once back in spare crew I would spend as much time as I could swimming and snorkeling, trying to soak up some sun and get a tan. Most off duty evenings would be spent in the Great War bar, a submariners haunt – as I remember it was the first bar you would come to after crossing Manoel Island bridge, from the base. It wasn't far to stagger back to my camp bed aboard Ausonia afterwards.

The Cuban Missile Crisis – a run do.

23rd October 1962 – my 23rd Birthday.

Lower deck tradition, etiquette, misguided sense of friendship, the band of brothers syndrome, against rules and regulations and good sense, had me invited around the messes at 'up spirits'. My watch keeping duties were covered, leaving me free to sleep off the effects of the celebration – or so I thought!

I had barely been akip for half an hour when I was being shaken roughly. It took a while to sink into my muzzy brain what I was being told. "We're going back in to store for war". Sure enough it wasn't long before we were at Misida Creek, Malta, off-loading those fish (torpedoes) fitted with blowing heads and replacing with others fitted with warheads.

I could not be left to condense snot in my fore-ends bunk, all the bunks had to be dismantled while work was in progress. All hands not employed loading torpedoes were required to take on all other stores needed for what could be an extended patrol. I knew what this involved having experienced preparing for 'mystery tours' at Faslane.

The many boxes we loaded formed a false deck, another obstacle for us to clamber over. The Jimmy had much to calculate, then direct the chief stoker how much water to put in or take out of the compensating tanks.

I knew that Cuba had been discovered by one of my boyhood heroes, Christopher Columbus, in 1492. Its recent history to my mind showed a failure of U.S. policy, how the wealthiest super power could allow such a close neighbour not to get a fair deal from the U.S. companies that owned a large proportion of Cuba's sugar plantations and who imported much of Cuba's tobacco products. I think it was a result of America's shortsightedness that opened the door to a corrupt dictatorship and then its overthrow by the young lawyer Fidel Castro. The U.S, opposed to Castro's left wing policies, forced him to turn to the Soviet Union.

In 1961 Cuban exiles in the U.S, backed by the CIA, attempted an invasion at the Bay of Pigs. This was a fiasco and was easily defeated by Castro. This is my simplification of a complex history, but I believe this led to the Soviets installing a nuclear missile base on America' own doorstep. As I was supping rum, Soviet transports were en route to Cuba with missiles and warheads.

JFK, the American president at the time, issued an ultimatum to the Soviet Union, turn the ships around and dismantle the bases or we will destroy them. The possibility of nuclear conflict and world war three loomed large. It was very inconsiderate to do this on my birthday!

My knowledge of naval strategy is very basic, but I know that Sevastopol, in the Crimea, is the headquarters of the Soviet Black Sea fleet and the main base of its ships that operate in the Mediterranean. Their submarines are based close by at Balaklava.

To enter the Mediterranean they must sail through the Bosporus and the Sea of Marmara into the Dardanelles and down the Aegean.

One would imagine that the Russians, the masters of chess, would have set up their board in anticipation, rather than have them bottled up in the Black Sea. They did have a few submarines based on a tender at Valona, Albania, but these had been withdrawn in 1961 when Albania broke relations with Moscow and withdrew from the Warsaw Pact. For any of their ships and submarines already in the Mediterranean to get out into the Atlantic, they would have to try and force the Straits of Gibraltar. Britain has not held on to the rock all these years as a tourist destination. As I had joined this submarine from spare crew, my duties did not include me being yeoman to the navigator, so I did not have access to the charts. As it should be, things were on a need to know basis. The captain would announce what he thought we needed to know once he thought we needed to know it.

What I did know was that much of my time would be spent operating what we called 'shuff duff'. Unlike radar, this was a passive device. It did not transmit, so its use was not detectable. We would gain details of the frequency and pulse repetition rate of any radar set being operated in our vicinity. From these details we could tell the type of radar and its use, for instance, navigation, surface search, air warning or missile direction. Each had a NATO code name, some of which I still remember, snoop light and snoop plate were on their Foxtrot and Zulu class submarines, pot drum and pot head on destroyers and cruisers, these were all surface search radars. Knife rest and big net were air warning radars.

Shuff duff was essential while we were snorting. We had to be able to detect their anti-submarine aircrafts' radar which would be searching for our presence before they homed in on our snort head and came in to attack. It would give us literally minutes to break the charge and get to a safe depth – hopefully.

The opposition would be taking similar defensive measures and wherever our ships operated their 'Elint' intelligence gathering ships would invariably turn up. Therefore we were always interested in their movements. It was a case of spies spying on spies. Fortunately good sense prevailed. The Soviets backed down and war was averted, but it did spoil my birthday!

It was not until 1971 that the Russians made an agreement with Syria to use the port of Tartus as a logistics support base for their Black Sea fleet. This was achieved by writing off Syria's arms debts accrued during the Soviet era. The base has three floating docks. It is now being converted, as a permanent base, for Russia's nuclear armed warships, aircraft carriers and nuclear missile submarines.

The Cuban Missile Crisis
— a run do.

Back to Tiptoe and life as a married man

I had leave owing so I flew back to the UK to spend Christmas 1962 with my then girl friend at her family home. I was due to fly back to Malta the day after Boxing Day, but heavy snow fell. My plane, a Vickers Vanguard taxied out to Heathrow's runway, she revved up then thought twice and returned to the terminal, problems with de-icing. We spent the night in a nearby hotel then, in the morning boarded a Vickers Viscount to fly back to Malta.

The snow lay on the ground in the UK until March. My letters to my girlfriend, describing the heat and sunshine, made her determined to join me in Malta for a sunshine holiday. In the meantime I was posted to Tiptoe as permanent crew as she was coming to the end of her re-fit.

The majority of her new crew were already in Malta on married accompanied postings. Initially only three of us were single men. We were accommodated and victualed at HMS St Angelo, a fort which dates back to the Knights of Malta. It is built on a hill overlooking Valetta harbour. We would travel to and from dockyard creek, where the submarine lay in the dock, by Dghajsa, a light wooden boat propelled by a single stern oar, retained by the Navy as water taxis they criss crossed the various creeks and inlets.

The regular Navy at St Angelo left us alone. We lived right at the summit of the hill, in what was called a catacomb, the thick walls had burial plaques high up bearing the names and coats of arms of those interred within the walls. Right outside our door was an area enclosed with railings, apparently a mass grave for victims of a bygone plague. The whole place was rather spooky, ok when all three of us went ashore together, not so the night I was on a 'stand by' duty.

I had to remain at St Angelo on call for whatever emergency might happen. The other two as usual went off to the bright lights. I eventually got to sleep but awoke in fright in the early hours. Strange wailing noises were coming from the dark area where a tunnel led up to within the walls. It was of course the two un-holy ghosts, 'Scrobie' and 'Slinger', full of alcoholic spirits, trying to test my nerve. I failed miserably.

Tiptoe's new captain had not yet been appointed, or at least if he had been he had not yet taken command. The first lieutenant, Lt. Holliday, was a great motivator of men and a time and motion expert. He had calculated that if we chipped and painted an area within two frames of the inside of the hull per day the job would be completed well within time.

It would be job and finish. We started early before the heat of the sun. The noise of massed 'windy hammers' reverberating inside the hull was like the start of the 'Indy 500'. I guarantee I was back at St Angelo's bar terrace, drinking beer and planning the afternoon and evening action plan by midday, daily.

Lt. Holliday had recommended me for training as a Special Duties Officer, but this would be quite a bit down the line, as I had a number of hurdles to jump before this could happen. In the meantime I had to sort out where my girlfriend would stay when she came out for her holiday. To the rescue came Enid Bray (her husband, Bill 'Donkey' Bray had served with me aboard Tudor). They leased a spacious flat overlooking

Sliema Creek and they had a spare bedroom.

It was late May when she came out. The time flew by after that as we were busy sightseeing and socializing. As the end of her holiday loomed, we thought why not get married here. We knew that, once back in the UK, I could be posted anywhere in the world within a short time. Also, money was tight due to low pay and the carefree lifestyle I led. I had some long term savings but was not able to touch them. Tiptoe was due to return to the UK in October and once we were married, Jan could return to the UK courtesy of the RAF just before then, along with the other wives.

Once the crew got wind of our intentions things seemed to take on their own momentum and we had a lot of arrangements to make in a short space of time. The Reverend John Oliver, Naval Chaplain aboard HMS Ausonia, agreed to conduct the wedding service at the Holy Trinity Church, Sliema. We set the date for the 6th of July. The banns were called aboard Ausonia on 9th June at Malta, 16th June at Marseille, and 23rd June at Gibraltar.

Happy go lucky, John (Blossom) Flower was to be my best man. John and his wife, Barbara, had been very supportive to both of us, as were 'Dusty' and Pat Miller. Dusty was one of a very few in those days that owned his own car. With him as chauffeur, we would use his ornate Zephyr Zodiac as the wedding car. They gave us the use of their spacious flat in which to hold the wedding buffet. Pat baked and iced the wedding cake and Lieutenant Holliday loaned us his ceremonial sword with which to dismember it.

One of Tiptoe's sparkers, Dave Whitton, had been a professional photographer in civie street. He took an excellent set of photographs which he presented to us in an album. During our nearly 50 years of marriage anyone that has seen the photos has commented on their superb quality.

It was to be a real white wedding. Blossom and I would be in full white tropical uniform, the bride would wear a dress of white Maltese lace.

The day of our wedding was special but seemed slightly surreal to me and I only remember it in snapshots, little incidents that happened during the day. Mid-morning, along with Scrobie and Slinger, was spent in the hairdressers shop along the Strand at Sliema. No old style Sweeney Todd the barber. Here girl hairdressers, knowing this was my big day, were laughing and joking while cutting and shaping my 'Tony Curtis' with a Boston at the nape of the neck – all the rage in those days.

The three of us went for our final drinks as a trio of single lads to the Great War bar – not a glitzy place like the Bamboo a couple of doors away along Sliema front – just a bar, spit and sawdust, without the sawdust. Jose kept his beer cold, his glasses clean and always feigned an interest in our sometimes incoherent burblings, keeping the bar open on many an occasion until we fell off our stools. Today he toasted my future happiness and wouldn't take any money.

I left the bar in good time to change into my tropical whites and get to the church, to join up with my best man and await my bride. She looked stunning as she appeared at my side. The service passed in a blur, I couldn't get over the number of people in the church, the crew members and their wives and children.

So much work had been done behind the scenes to make the day go perfectly and I don't remember thanking them all enough, I can only hope I did as it's too late now. The wedding car taking us to the reception had a 'before' board hung on the radiator and an 'after' board dangling from the boot – cartoon caricatures by some wag, these drew much attention from the crowded pavements and much hooting and honking from traffic on the roads. We both gave the royal wave as we drove by, feeling special – like royalty.

We went for a short honeymoon – well very short, just one night in an hotel at St Pauls Bay. At first we were shown to an attic room instead of the bridal suite we were expecting. It was my shipmates' version of an upgrade. By the time we eventually hit the mattress I was too tired to comply with the request in the telegram signed 'Crew Tiptoe': "Report position, speed, depth and nature of bottom at midnight. Proceed dived to lower half of area for endurance trials. Weather cloudy, maybe little sun later, dress optional oilskins. Congratulations and good luck on your future exercises", or that from my brother John aboard S.S. 'Gulf Scot' who cabled via Portishead radio "Orders run submerged until batteries exhausted". I think I was asleep as soon as my head hit the pillow.

Tomorrow we would go to the small flat we had hired at Gzira, Paula. The rest of our stay in Malta would be a long honeymoon until the time came for Tiptoe to sail back to Gosport. My wife would return home along with many of the other wives and their children aboard an RAF Comet, having applied for an 'indulgence flight' as they were known. The cost about 30 shillings (£1.50 in today's decimal currency), that was to pay for refreshments during the flight. The plane would land at RAF Lyneham, a short train ride to her family home. I waved her off at RAF Luqua and eventually she would meet me at Gosport, when the submarine arrived home about three weeks later.

Above us the waves and below a cake of many layers

Leaving aside the very deep trenches you could take as a very rough average that the world's oceans have a depth of 12,000 feet and the seas about 7,000 feet, so if you consider that the deepest diving submarines would not be operating much below 1,000 feet and most not much below 500 feet, you could say that we were in effect only scratching the surface. The quest has been to build submarines to operate deeper using lighter, stronger materials and modern construction methods. Unlike research vessels which can be constructed in a spherical shape, where sea pressure is evenly distributed, the most practical shape is a cylinder with domed ends. The submarine for naval purposes has to be mobile and agile able to deploy its weapons and intelligence gathering systems throughout the vast areas of the world's oceans.

The majority of these systems as well as the submarine operating equipment require outlets through the pressure hull. Some of these are massive like the hatches, usually five in number, the torpedo tubes, snort induction and propeller shafts. Others perhaps not so large, the periscopes, radar, communications and intelligence masts as well as the mass of high and low pressure air, telemotor and oleo lines and cables to operate rudder, hydroplanes, the capstan, sonar, the log, echo sounder, underwater telephone and the gun if fitted. Without making any more of a detailed list these should be enough to make any non-submariner aware of the potential weaknesses of this pressure hull.

Sea pressure in lbs per sq.inch is approximately half the depth in feet so it doesn't take much working out to find what these outlets have to contend with. Valves are fitted to all inlet and discharge pipes to allow them to be shut off when going deep or under attack. The hull is originally designed with a 70% margin of safety over the normal maximum diving depth, but age and resulting hull deterioration may limit this factor. I have served on boats where we were limited to 250ft, no one mentioned what safety factor was calculated below this depth, possibly just as well for peace of mind.

Being able to dive deeper has obvious advantages, apart from putting vertical distance between ourselves and any shallow set explosive charges it allows time to correct any loss of control suffered because of it.

On arrival at our patrol area or awaiting arrival of potential targets that 'intelligence' has said that we might expect to pass through our patch, the Captain would go deep to take a bathythermograph reading. This would give him an insight into the nature of the ocean below and in particular the depth of any layer of denser salinity he may be able to use as a shield from the searching sonar of escort ships carrying out a retaliatory attack. This layer could help by deflecting or absorbing energy from the sonar's beam. Here again the ability to dive deeper would increase the possibility of us using this tactic.

The clarity of water in the Mediterranean, especially in sunlight, was a contributing factor to many of our submarine losses in that theatre of operations during World War II. A submarine's outline could be spotted by searching aircraft at shallow and not so shallow depths, so being able to dive deeper was an asset in this regard also. In sea areas surrounding coasts, notably in the northern Mediterranean where I had experience, where rivers can disgorge vast amounts of fresh water into the sea, especially in times of snow melt or after heavy rainfall, a submarine can suddenly and quickly lose depth when traversing these areas and obviously trim has to be adjusted to maintain desired depth. This sudden loss of depth control can be more than just a mere nuisance if in shallow water without much depth under the keel, or if snorting at the time, whatever the depth.

The fresh water, being lighter, floats and stays nearer the surface, whereas the heavier seawater, dense with salinity, will sink and may form a layer below. Temperature and salinity both play a part. Ocean waters get denser as the temperature goes down, so the colder the water the more dense it becomes and the greater the salinity. Two layers of water with the same salinity, the warmer water will float on top of the colder water, however temperature has a greater effect on the density of water than does salinity thus a layer of water with higher salinity and higher temperature can float on top of water with lower salinity. Interpreting bathythermograph readings was for those above my intellect and rank so I have only mentioned it in general terms.

When discussing this layered cake, the medium in which we lived and worked, the 'oggin' as we called it, one must consider the effects of the surface currents and circulation as well as deep water currents. One submarine, the 'Alliance', which I have mentioned later in this book took part in investigations into these ocean currents.

It was these ocean currents, following the prevailing wind direction, which took a hand in enabling the lifeboat my father and others of the crew of S.S. Quebec City had taken to after the sinking by U-boat of the ship, to reach proximity to the coast of Sierra Leone where they were rescued by an R.N. destroyer.

Apart from these surface currents there are those deeper currents which form what is known as the global conveyor belt which oceanographers say takes a thousand years to complete its cycle. Temperature plays a major part in all of this. My simple understanding is that it is a reaction to solar heating of water close to the equator. Here the ocean is about 8 centimeters higher than in mid-latitudes causing a slight slope which water wants to flow down and then cooling in polar regions and of course the effect of water being drawn in to replace water lifted by heat or that sunk by cold.

It would hurt my brain to delve any deeper into the subject. I have called the sea a cake of many layers, most of which have yet to be fully explored or exploited, but I'm sure with need for minerals and food sources it will be.

The Queen, God bless her.

Matelots have been known to grumble about politicians, the admiralty, their skipper or coxswain and anyone else who was not there to defend themselves. The only person matelots, and probably most other servicemen, don't moan about, is the reigning monarch – in this case the Queen. After all, we signed up to serve Queen and country, rather than the incumbent government of whatever hue, governments could come and go.

The Queen, God Bless Her – it was in large brass letters around the wooden circumference of the rum barrel of a large ship or shore establishment. The toast would be "The Queen" our reply "God bless her". Rum had been issued in the Royal Navy since 1665 and didn't cease being issued until shortly after I left the Navy. 31st July 1970 was a sad day for the Navy. I couldn't imagine life aboard ship without it.

It was a privilege we had and officers didn't and it was one that could be taken away as a punishment. 'Up spirits' was a social time, more so in harbour when for half an hour or so its warming glow could make one forget the friction and fractions of our often uncomfortable existence.

The rum itself was a blend of fine rums 95.5 proof, or 54.6 alcohol, strong. The issue per man 1/8th of a pint (half a gill). Rum issued to junior rates was mixed with water and known as 'grog'.[1] In general service and shore bases the mixture was two parts water to one part rum, which we called 'two and one'. Aboard submarines we normally had it mixed 'one and one'. Whichever way, it was pleasant. The reason for the water was to stop us bottling and saving it. Chiefs and P.O.'s could be trusted not to do that, so theirs was issued neat – but most took it with some water. The issue was a ritual and strictly controlled, those 'under age' having not reached the age of twenty, were excluded from the mess.

Once I reached age twenty I never met seas rough enough to stop me drinking my rum and I had been in some right hooligans. The warming tot, when coming below from being strapped in on the bridge, in the teeth of an arctic gale, could make one feel almost human again.

There were times when the signal 'splice the mainbrace'[2] was sent around the fleet, a new monarch crowned, a royal wedding or birth, an inspection of the fleet by the monarch. This never happened during my time, but it was an extra issue of a tot per man.

Three times I had an extra tot authorized by the Captain, after working 'up top' in bad weather, always appreciated, it was like a badge of honour.

---

[1]Admiral Vernon, known in the Navy as 'Old Grog' ordered the mixing of water into the rum back in 1740.

[2]The mainbrace, that part of a sailing ship's rigging which supported the main sails, was a priority target used by an enemy to disable the ship. Its subsequent re-splicing by the best seaman was rewarded by this extra tot.

Skirmishes along squeeze gut alley

The alley lay between Gosport High Street and Pneumonia Bridge, then a walkway crossing Haslar Creek. This was the returning route for matelots, mainly submariners, but also those general service rates of HMS Dolphin, HMS Hornet and Royal Naval Hospital Haslar.

Its name was derived from the combined effects of its 'fry-up' foods (fish 'n' chips, sausage 'n' chips, fried egg banjos, etc. etc) and the liquid intake of Brickwoods products with a bit of scrumpy thrown in – or thrown up which was often the case. Some of the Royal Navy's more infamous battles have occurred here. Local residents were not best pleased, nor were the local police.

The Navy could not send a gunboat to sort it out, but they sent what they thought the next best thing – the shore patrol. It was like sending a red rag to pacify a bull. The regular 'crushers' as we called the regulating branch, had their hands full, containing the Saturday night battles of Pompey and the NAAFI Club. Ours in Gosport were a mere sideshow in comparison, a flea bite on an elephant's arse.

It had been a cold winter while I was spare crew and like most I would stop at the 'greasy spoon' for a hand held banquet to warm me while traversing the creek over the open-railed Pneumonia Bridge. I rarely used pubs on the Gosport side, preferring the NAAFI Club, its cheaper beer

252

and its proximity to the Wrens' nest. By the time I'd caught the last ferry and got my grub along Squeeze Gut Alley, my bunk would be calling me, although one couldn't always account for the company one found himself in. As you may know sometimes the mildest mannered could turn into a raging bull with a mix of drinks inside him and you may have to protect yourself, or others, from him.

It was later, while doing a short, submarine radar course, that I heard stories of 'juke box being hurled from a pub window', 'fights and scuffles in the High Street', 'food not being paid for'. All this usually happened Friday and Saturday evenings.

I was lumbered to be on the shore patrol a couple of times during this period. The patrol consisted of a killik and two. I was one of the two, being an A.B. at the time. The other one of the two was Geordie, a chef, who when ashore himself had the reputation as a miscreant. The killik, an older three badgeman, so called because of the three good conduct stripes on his arm, didn't fill me with confidence. He told me how he dealt with fights. He said "I always go for the one who looks like he's losing, he's always pleased to be handcuffed and the more dangerous one, the one who's winning, is then less likely to attack the patrol". "All well and good, stripey" said I, "but looking at your face, it doesn't look like that strategy often works". Stripey had a bent nose, a scar through one eyebrow and teeth like a NAAFI piano - one black, one white and one missing.

We dressed in No.3's with white belt and gaiters, the white R.N. shore patrol armband, making us an easily identifiable target. We each had a night stick (long truncheon) hanging from the belt, though none of us would want to use it on 'one of our own'. The early part of the evening was quiet, this particular time. We got ourselves fish and chips and huddled in a doorway out of sight. The local police panda car would call by a couple of times and we would chat to the coppers, one of whom was an ex-RAF policeman. They would then park up near the ferry terminal.

After last orders were called things got busier. We tried to quieten down the singers and chanters and move the congregators through the alley. There was one real troublemaker, a 'scouser' who was well known to stripey. They had crossed swords in the past. Usually a popular bloke but tonight he wanted to take on the world. Well not actually the world as much as two general service ratings who scouser insisted were the very same storemen who wouldn't let him have a pair of new steaming boots unless he took the worn out ones back.

Looking at the badges on the right arms of these two I could see that they were sick bay 'tiffies' (or scablifters) as we called the medical branch – probably from R.N.H. Haslar. We couldn't get that through to scouser. He was listening to no one, least of all to 'turncoats' as he kept calling us. We couldn't let him stagger back over the bridge amongst the general service sailors and the two scablifters in particular.

In the end we cuffed him to 'geordie', called the panda car and sent him round to be released half a mile from Dolphin main gate so he could stagger back on his own.

I was pleased when the tili' arrived to take us back to the main gate, where we enjoyed a hot cup of 'ki' while stripey made out his patrol report to the quartermaster.

Mentioning the tili', which is what we called the Bedford Dormobile Utilicon used by the Navy as a general purpose people carrier, reminds me of this ditty that girls of the W.R.N.S, the wrens, used to sing:-

> Our chief wren said follow the men
>
> And don't dilly dally on the way

Off went the tili' with the chief wren in it,

I followed on with a sub-lieutenant

But I dillied and dallied, dallied and dillied

Lost my way and don't know where to roam

But you can't trust a subby like a three badged stoker

When you can't find your way home.

Choke points and Chimps

In the Navy I did not venture east of Hong Kong, or to Australia, New Zealand, Japan, nor to any of the Pacific islands, nor to the west coast of South or North America, and not to any part of Canada. I'd not been to Russia, although I may have trespassed their territorial waters on the odd occasion. (I've been to some of these places since the Navy, but not during my service). But show me the submariner that's never been to either Scotland or Northern Ireland and I will show you a fresh water kipper.

Crossing an ocean in a submarine was a slog but without much danger, nor was being below about 120ft. That was our comfort zone and usually not much to write home about or fill a page of a book with, for that matter. Negotiating the lochs and the rocks, the busy Clyde and fishing boats – especially ones trailing nets - was another matter. Leaving Pompey harbour through the Solent and the Needles without swamping a yacht or a close call with a ferry was an art. These choke points were the main hazard and I would be busy at my office – the radar shack.

You have to realize that there was no radar P.P.I. (plan position indicator, not unlike an orange glowing television) on the bridge for the Captain or Officer of the watch to consult as on any normal ship. Therefore, he up top had to rely on the contact reports the radar operator passed over the intercom. This particular choke point or navigational hazard was the River Foyle leaving Londonderry (or Derry according to your persuasion). This fast flowing river emptied into Lough Foyle, it was about 30 miles or so before we could clear Magilligan Point and pass Inishowen Head before turning to port into deep water to the north of Malin Head where we would be in our comfort zone, or relatively so anyway.

Special sea dutymen, the most experienced of each department, were closed up, normal routine for leaving any harbour. I was at my post – the radar shack, a small cubby hole, just enough room for me on my seat in front of the set, a grey painted intercom on its adjustable arm in front of my face. I kept the sliding door shut usually to block out noise from the engine room and to keep sightseers away. It was ok normally to have an oily leaning over your shoulder, but not when leaving harbour.

It was a day with patchy fog and low visibility. Nothing would stop our intrepid skipper, or any other, they all came out of the same mould. You can't play chess without the pawns being in place and as long as the Royal Navy's pawns and rooks (we had no bishops) were in place it didn't matter to him if anyone else's Navy turned up or not.

Outside the fog must have clamped down. I wouldn't have known except my door slid open and the navigator's bearded face peered over my shoulder from the passageway outside. He was watching the same blobs on the screen that I was watching and reporting to the captain on the bridge. He would be able to make no other interpretation than me, notwithstanding his greater brain power. To give him his due he made no comment, but I understood, without it being said, that their lordships would not have been happy just having it rest on the view of a killick R.P.2 should we collide with one of these blobs. I was more familiar with these blobs, they were my bread and butter day in, day out. They do say that you can train a chimp to do most things, but I doubt that he could tell you what these blobs would turn out to be – well I couldn't anyway. Were they a buoy or a boat? Didn't matter too much, as long as whatever it was was stationary. Fortunately not much else was moving although I was told that on the bridge they could hear other foghorns. We had our watertight compartments shut off and were still propelling on main motors so we could go astern if needed.

I was aware of nothing, just riveted to my screen, talking into my mike to the unseen captain, his voice giving a curt "Roger radar" to my bearing reports. A blob would detach itself from the clutter caused by a bend in the river ahead and move left or right, hopefully, down my screen. I'd mark its position with a chinagraph pencil on the screen. If the bearing remained steady it would be more of a problem. Often the blob would float past unseen, either through a natural course of events or the skipper had jockied our course and it would merge with the ground clutter or join up with the bigger blob of a headland or whatever. Modern radars (not that I've ever used one) are much more discerning than what we had then. I think it took about two and a half hours to clear the river this particular time, or at least before the fog had lifted enough for special sea dutymen to fall out. My relief slid open the door and I almost fell out. You could have wrung me out like a dish cloth. He took over my seat, I passed him a 'sitrep' made sure he was up to speed and staggered forward to the mess.

The rest of the special sea dutymen would be doing the same, the signalman from the bridge, the coxswain off of the wheel, the telegraphsman and others from other parts of the boat. Luckily my watch was not due on at the moment, otherwise I would have had to juggle the watches a bit and put one of the R.P.3's on for a while until I felt able to focus my eyes which were out like organ stops.

The skipper passed "Well done radar" through the medium of the navigator. It made life seem worthwhile for a time.

Good-Will hsit to Hull

Visits to ports in northern England were popular with matelots. They have a great tradition of working men's clubs and Hull was no exception. The beer up north in those days seemed to be superior to that down south and we were always made welcome by the club members. Many of them were from the fishing fleets so they understood better than anyone how uncomfortable life at sea could be. When fishing was good so were their wages and they were generous to us poorly paid souls. We tried to repay them by entertaining their wives, girlfriends and daughters.

My main memory of Hull concerns the range of the tides. Unlike Naval dockyards there were no surrounding wall or wire fences around the jetty in fact half a mile away was the nearest pub. As duty leading hand one of my duties was to organize a rota to cover what was known as the trot sentry. Prior to the threat of the IRA and other terrorists the sentry would not be armed in home ports, except for Northern Ireland where he would carry a sten or lanchester carbine. He was responsible for the security of the boat and its moorings, as well as assisting those returning from shore, most with a skin full of booze, to negotiate the gangway, hatch and steep ladder. The secret was to get them turned in their bunks without too much disturbance. Disturbing the duty officer and getting him involved was best avoided, better he spent his time worrying about what the Russian Navy were up to rather than his own bunch of miscreants.

The lure of the pub was too great for some of the lads. I relented a bit by sending two of them up with the mess fanny to fill with beer on condition they only had a quick pint themselves. They no doubt managed to down a couple but it was not long before they came back along the jetty lugging the full aluminium fanny. It should have caused no problem, not much more than a pint and a half per person – if all had their share.

I turned in at about 2300hrs as I would be doing my stint from 0500hrs to 0700hrs as trot sentry. All was well until at about 0100hrs an engine room tiffy, returning from shore, found he could hardly climb down the gangplank, it was almost perpendicular. 'Dodger' Long the trot sentry was dozing and hadn't eased the gangplank's lashings as the tide fell. Worse than that neither had he eased the fore and after breast ropes or the wire rope springs. The ropes being nylon had a lot of stretch in them, not so the springs. I don't know how much further the tide had to fall and as they already had the weight of the boat something would soon have to give.

Let me just explain. The fore spring led from a pair of bollards on the forecasing to a bollard on the jetty about level with our engine room hatch, aft of the bridge. The after spring led from a similar pair of bollards on the after casing to a bollard on the jetty about level with our escape hatch, on our fore casing. Their purpose was to prevent fore and aft movement, thus we stayed at the same position relative to the jetty.

Dodger knew he couldn't do the job alone so he shook me to give me the good news. I said "Oh dear, it's a good job it was a tiffy and not an officer" or something like that. Our duty officer was due to be called at

0200hrs to do his rounds. I was worried I could lose my hook over this and they would probably string Dodger up. The taut springs worried me as they were leading up at an angle and trapping the figure of eight turns around the bollards. I got the rest of the seamen up from their bunks as I wanted two men at each of the bollards. We had to try to ease them out together, if we could, to avoid just one bearing all the weight. Between us we managed – I was sweating, despite it being a cold night, as it created a lot of shuddering jolts as we eased them out. Luckily the duty officer slept through it all and everything was shipshape and Bristol fashion, as they say, when he was woken with a cup of tea to do his rounds.

It cost Dodger his next day's tot to repay the engine room tiff and for the next few days we all claimed a gulpers from him. (Favours in the Navy were repaid on a sliding scale depending on their magnitude, either full tot, half a tot, gulpers or sippers. Sometimes it would be a case of bargaining, at a time like this it would be demanded.)

Where do you Think you are, your daddy's yacht?

Red watch seamen were sitting round the mess tables – well it was like one long table cut in half by a narrow walkway, to allow mess members to move in or out of the mess without disturbing the whole row of those seated along both sides. Rarely could the members of two watches remain undisturbed for very long.

At this moment, white watch had left the mess, having drunk their tot of rum, to relieve their opposite numbers of blue watch so they could come forward and have theirs. That is except for the torpedoman, he had to come aft to the mess. His was a lonely duty in the fore-ends, not much for him to do at watch diving, except if he had to fire smoke candles from the SSE (submerged signal ejector) or replace a candle in the oxygen generator. This had a heater element atop the burning chamber, to start the sodium chlorate/iron filings mixture in the candle burning. This at least helped to replace some of the oxygen we were breathing in. Close to the forward mess we also had a CO_2 absorption unit which sucked air from the ventilation trunking, through a soda lime canister. The fore-endsman, or one of us in the mess, would change the canister as necessary.

We, of the red watch, would have a brainstorming session helped by the warming glow imparted by the rum, having about 15 minutes while the blues had their tots, before we went down to the galley to bring the messdishes of dinner to the mess.

Jock Brodie, normally a dour taciturn character, was sounding off "D'ya ken that bloody wee geordie scablifter fra' Guzz, bloody barrack stancheon, wee gob shite". Veejay Chakrabarti (we called him 'Jack Rabbit') Indian Navy trainee submarine sonarman, turned to me and asked if anyone here spoke English apart from him. "No, only you and me mate" said I "You've only got that wingeing taffy sheepshagger, the oggie yaffler, scouser and that nutter from Glasgow who keeps on about that sickbay tiffy who told him he's fit for duty, but to keep his dressing clean, they're the sum total of our watch apart from yours truly and yourself".

"Goodness gracious me" said Jack Rabbit (I think he'd been listening to Peter Sellers). "Yes Jack" said I, "They'll spend the next four weeks slagging each other and anyone else, but once the hatches are open we'll all be over the gangplank and in the nearest bar together, you included". "I don't drink" said Jack Rabbit. "You soon will" said I – and do you know what, I was right. Shame really 'cos I used to have half his tot every day.

We were the oldest boat in the squadron and had the most junior of skippers, seniority wise. As such we were accorded the privilege of the most far flung patrol area. We had sailed about six hours before the boat in the area adjacent to ours and consequently we would arrive back to base six hours or so after them. It was not unknown to arrive at our start point and be told "Weather's too bad for the flyboys to fly" or "The convoy you were to attack has been diverted", or perhaps to be told nothing, so we'd just wait, stoogeing about in an empty sea, just us and an occasional albatross. As an albatross has more sense than to inhabit the north Atlantic the occasional bird was probably a gannet, but whatever it was, we were out there.

Still, as the coxswain would say "Where do you think you are, your

daddy's yacht? If you can't take a joke you shouldn't have joined". That put everything right for us and in context. He was sent to us as a disciple for their lordships and was a very wise man. He was the original conservationist, he issued just the bare regulation food ration and very little spillage allowance with the rum ration, just in case our patrol would be extended for another six months or so. He would surely go to heaven.

Now and again either myself or the bunting tosser would attend the after exercise 'wash-up', carrying the control room log book and relevant charts and plots for the navigator. After this particular NATO exercise the four ring Captain of the anti-submarine flotilla rose to his feet to expound the successes of his escort group. He was, however, soon deflated by our most junior C.O. who, referring to our log said "You zigged in position so and so, you zagged at position so and so at such and such a time and I've got periscope photos of your ship and of the tanker you were escorting, also you failed to acknowledge my smoke signals".

I heard no congratulation from the escort commander on our success, I only detected a certain iciness. Sometimes it was hard to remember that we were on the same side, against a Warsaw Pact hell bent on world domination – or so they said. Still it kept us all employed, steaming about using up resources. Mind you, our coxswain did save a few tins of paste, some bangers and a couple of tots for the good of the world.

By the time Jack Rabbit returned to India, he drank like a fish and spoke a mixture of gorbals slang, coupled with geordie cum scouse humour, in a sing song Welsh lilt!

Pirates of Penzance

We were pleased to enter the sheltered waters of Falmouth harbour. We had surfaced out in deep water to the south west of Lizard Point. We knew it was going to be rough up top. The storm had been brewing up. We had trouble snorting the previous night trying to get a charge in our waning batteries. The snort valve is designed to shut when immersed, causing the pounding diesels to suck their air supply from inside the boat. This obviously causes a vacuum making eardrums pop and sleep almost impossible. If the vacuum reaches a potentially dangerous level the charge is broken, main engines are stopped, the boat is re-trimmed to ensure easier depth keeping and then snorting is resumed.

Preparing to surface in rough weather an 'elephant's foot', a canvas tube, is fitted around the conning tower ladder. This has an access slit near its foot to allow the officer of the watch and the lookout to enter and climb the ladder. The 'bird bath' which is a large circular canvas trough is rigged so that the ladder and its surrounding canvas tube stand within it. Their purpose is to capture any seawater pouring down the hatch when seas swamp the bridge. A suction hose is led into the bird bath allowing the captured water to be pumped out.

Just prior to surfacing the tannoy message throughout the boat "Stand by for heavy rolling" reaffirms what we already know.

The boat steers into the heavy seas, main ballasts are **blown** using plenty of air. The Captain allows the upper hatch to break surface completely before ordering the lid to be opened. The boat tends to wallow before gaining full buoyancy. This can be dangerous for the bridge crew and they have to be ready to slam the hatch shut and stand on it while holding their breath should the seas swamp the bridge. The low pressure blower is run, as needed, to maintain buoyancy and the split **blow** can be used to correct any list.

On this occasion the skipper kept us heading into the seas all night before deeming it safe enough at daybreak to gradually turn the boat across the seas and point the bows toward our desired destination – Falmouth.

The visibility was good and every time the boat lifted on the following sea every ship for miles could be clearly seen. For this reason we were not operating seaguard radar and would not until we got closer in to the south west approaches.

When it was time for our watch to take over I elected to relieve the lookout, rather than the helmsman as I knew it wouldn't be long before I found myself in the confines of the radar shack once 'special sea dutymen' were closed up ready for entering harbour.

I collected a dry penguin suit from the engine room then called up the voice pipe and received permission to relieve the lookout. I climbed over the side of the bird bath and through the opening of the trunk and hauled myself up the ladder against the howling inrush of air and spray being sucked through the hatch above my head by the pounding diesels in the engine room I had just left.

I heaved myself through the hatch and onto the bridge platform just as one of the following seas broke over the back of the bridge and cascaded over the three of us. I took over the lookout's binoculars as he pointed out the various ships and fishing boats that were visible. He unstrapped his harness and passed it to me before disappearing down the hatch to dry off and turn in.

The officer of the watch was an R.N.R. Lieutenant a merchant mariner from a Fyffes Banana ship. He was quite an experienced submariner. We would normally have a good conversation, but today we only spoke if I reported a new sighting to him. An hour later I was pleased to be relieved to return to the relative comfort of the control room to spend the next hour fighting to steer a straight course at the wheel.

We would spend the next two days alongside the jetty in Falmouth. Half the crew would be allowed ashore each afternoon until about 8.30 the next morning. The other half of the crew would be re-storing, re-loading and repairing.

Myself and three of my regular run ashore oppos went the first night. 'Mick' was the killik sparker (radio operator) not to be confused with sparks (the electrician). Mick, an Ulsterman, was the fastest morse sender I had ever seen. I sat with him many a time as he keyed off signals. He could recognize the keying actions of many of the operators on the other submarines that were strung out across the north atlantic or wherever else we were operating. If it happened to be someone he wasn't keen on, he would reel it off so fast that they had to keep asking for a repeat.

Hedley the outside killik stoker was a naturally funny fellow. He knew the submarine and its machinery inside out – he should do he spent most of his waking hours maintaining it. His sharp wit had upset many of his superiors throughout his career, engineer officers, captains and visiting admirals, it didn't matter to him. He'd been busted from P.O. and lost his hook (leading rate) twice. Along with the outside tiffy (artificer) he was responsible for all machinery outside of the engine room. My first week on the boat all I saw of Hedley was his steaming boots sticking out from under a ballast pump or condenser. He had spent a few months on my first boat (another old 'T' class similar to this one). He had warmed to me after the 'pedalo' incident, he said he had told the story in bars around the world's seaports. No doubt he had embellished the facts over the years. I have related the facts as I remember them earlier in this epistle.

The fourth member of the ugly bunch was 'Tansy' Lee the HSD. The killik sonar operator Tansy fancied himself as Gene Kruper, he loved to knock out a tune on bottles and glasses using a pair of old drumsticks he carried ashore with him.

We'd started our run ashore at midday after 'up spirits', drinking at one of Falmouth's lively bars. Tansy was in conversation with a ship chandler's driver who said he was going on to Penzance. Tansy once had a girlfriend there so he arranged that the four of us would pile in the man's van and go to search for her.

Once there we stumbled upon the Royal Hotel. Being out of season there were only a few regulars in the bar and not many guests at the hotel. What they thought of four of the Navy's finest clad in crumpled uniforms and reeking of diesel and mould didn't concern us. For the uninitiated when away from shore base or depot ship we had no means of taking a shower or dhobeying clothing. We only had a couple of handbasins, limited fresh water plus our toothbrushes.

After a couple of drinks Mick burst into song, his deep Irish voice melodious and sad. Tansy accompanied with drum solos on a row of wine glasses. Hearing the noise in the usually quiet bar the owner and his wife came down. It turned out that he had served in the Navy during the war as a P.O. steward. After intro's he asked if we minded if two of his hotel guests join us. They were two elderly ladies, one was Miss Wills of the tobacco family, the other was Lady Hewitt, wife of a former Lord Chief Justice. They joined in with the singing and joviality.

Later the hotel chef was summoned to cook for us and we were given rooms for the night. Before we retired to bed the ladies said they would send us back by car in the morning. They wanted us to return the next evening so they could treat us to a meal. We made our apologies explaining we would be on duty. Picture the looks we got as we tumbled out of the chauffer driven Rolls Royce looking a bit green about our gills as we arrived at the jetty.

Just before 'up spirits' we were summoned to see the coxswain. The hotel had called our first lieutenant requesting our presence for dinner. Jimmy refused as we were on duty. Within half an hour Admiralty in London had signaled Captain S/M at HMS Dolphin, he in turn signaled our Captain that we were to be picked up by car at 1630hrs. If our Captain needed spare crew to replace us they would be sent from Devonport. We knew all this before the coxswain and the Jimmy as Mick was taking down the signals. Needless to say they were seething.

The hotel dining room was laid up as if for a banquet. We had scrubbed and cleaned ourselves, having availed ourselves of the facilities aboard a passenger/cargo ship of the Port Line which had taken shelter in Falmouth and was moored ahead of us. Their generous crew allowed our lads to share their 'pig and whistle' bar as they called it.

We were introduced to other guests at the table, friends of the two ladies, and of the hotel owners. The food was wonderful as were the wines. It wasn't long before Mick was called upon to sing one of his sentimental songs. Tansy accompanied sounding as if he were playing a xylophone.

Miss Wills, knowing that I had been to Caracas, Venezuela, mentioned that she knew the British Consul there and when I said that I had met members of the consular staff she wanted to know all about it. You must bear in mind that in the years following the war and up until about 1960 most people didn't travel abroad for holidays. All eyes were on me as I said that as a boy I had followed the travels of Christopher Columbus the first westerner to sight Venezuela. I had read of Simon Bolivar and followed the adventures of the Spanish Conquistadors. One of my greatest ambitions I said was to follow in their footsteps along the course of the great Orinoko river exploring part of its 1,300 mile length.

A reception had been held for us in the grounds of the consulate and it was here I struck up a rapport with one of the staff, an ex Royal Marine corporal. He told me that he had heard of a secretive band of nomadic tribesmen living in the Llanos which are tropical grasslands that drain into the Orinoko. With the help of the consulate, leave was arranged for us both, as was transport to Guayana Highlands. We followed the river to the magnificent Angel Falls. As I was talking I noticed the old gentleman seated opposite me who I knew had spent many years in India with the colonial service. He was intent on my story, his eyes were glistening, no doubt reliving his days of adventure and exploration in India. He followed my every word as I told him how we made our way down from the scenic Highlands – hacking our way through tangles of creepers that dangled from towering trees and how we happened upon clumps of orchid-like flowers in their shade. We met various natives along our way, descendants of the ancient Aztecs. Two of them knew of the existence of the Fukawii, the band of pygmy-like Indians that roamed the Llanos. They agreed to lead us if we gave them our waterproof jackets

– which we found too hot for us to wear. They followed tracks in the tall pampas grass until in the distance we saw a disturbance in the grass as a number of heads and upper parts of small dark skinned men bobbed above its waving surface. Just as quickly they disappeared, until a few minutes later they bobbed up some fifty yards to our right. 'Fukawii' said one of the guides.

I paused in my story to take a drink as my throat was dry. As I looked around the table I noticed the whole of the dinner party were totally engrossed and awaiting my next words. Seeing me take a drink seemed to be the cue for them to do the same. Their drinks, even those of Mick and Hedley who had thirsts like Mongolian camels, had been untouched since my story began.

The old chap opposite me had been hacking as I swung my arm in sword-like slashes. He was swatting at mosquitoes the same time as me, I had brought his past adventures back to life. Thinking that I had better bring my story to a close before the old Indian hand had some sort of seizure, we realized, I said, that every time their heads broke surface they quickly scanned around and called something out in their high pitched reedy voices. Suddenly I reeled back as if in surprise, my audience were startled as I pointed my arm to the right. I cried out "Look six of them" wizened heads with copper earrings looping from their ears, small barbed spears clutched in their gnarled hands. As they rose above the waving grass they each called out "We're the fukawii, we're the fukawii".

Tansy had tumbled me and was anticipating some punch line because he'd been caught by me in the past. He started to laugh his peculiar whooping, wailing laugh. This soon became infectious, as starting with Mick and Hedley, one by one they realized the story was a figment of my warped drink fuelled imagination.

Lady Pamela and Miss Wills were almost crying and dabbing their eyes with dainty handkerchiefs. I glanced at the old Sahib across the table. He was still staring at the square of carpet my outstretched hand had pointed to, as if expecting the lost tribesmen to reappear.

Some months later back our the Dolphin base we were being inspected by Captain S/M when our skipper pointed me out to him and said "This is leading seaman Clarke sir". "Oh yes" said Captain S/M "Clarke of the Orinoko I presume". Sometimes it seems those in exalted positions do know what us mere mortals get up to!

Accidents and Misadventures

Very little happened by accident in the Andrew except an accident itself, as we had routines and procedures for most eventualities, tried and tested, updated if necessary. The submarine at the ripe old age of 21 was approaching the end of her final commission and was being used increasingly in the training role, taking to sea trainees of various specialties as part of their basic submarine training courses. Some of our own experienced crew members had been posted to attend promotion courses, or on promotion to other submarines and a couple went for nuclear training, their places being taken by Part 3 trainees who had just completed their own submarine training.

We were usually parked at what I think was known as no. 4 jetty, up toward Dolphin 2. It reminded me of the film 'Further up the Creek' with Frankie Howard and David Tomlinson, except we couldn't pass ourselves off as a luxury cruise liner, much less could we sell tickets for our trips. Tansy Lee said it reminded him of the poem 'Dobbin' about the old horse out at grass, turns his tail to the winds that pass. I remembered parts of the poem from schooldays and added "Something has happened, something is gone, the world is changing his work is done". We both agreed that the next step was the knackers yard, they'll make horse meat tins out of us.

In the same boat as us, metaphorically speaking that is, on the other side of the jetty lay another streamlined 'T' boat, the Tireless. She was carrying out a similar role to ourselves and also soon destined to meet the horsemeat tin maker. One slight difference was, when in harbour and as is normal, we didn't see much of our skipper, in fact we never saw him at all, whereas, the red haired, energetic C.O. of the Tireless seemed to often pop up and catch the unwary unawares. He was one Lt. Cdr 'Sandy' Woodward[1]. I can still picture him in my mind's eye striding along the jetty toward the two boats, under his arm a bulky black briefcase. Perhaps he was already planning his fleet dispositions for the Falklands campaign. I had just managed to alert Tireless's trot sentry before he was caught, clutching his mug of steaming tea. Our planning was good, unlike at the Falklands we had good airborne early warning systems.

Our captain was an entirely different personality. A little dour perhaps, showing little sense of humour, but then there was no need for comedy in his job, as submarine life is quite a serious business, though sometimes it seemed farcical and a comedy of errors. I did make him laugh one time. It was when he suggested we send a team to compete in a quiz competition over in Southsea. His friend, the skipper of the 'Finwhale' was sending a team. He had heard that a couple of us were part of a regular team at the White Hart in Gosport, but not that I only went

[1]Vice Admiral Sir John Forster (Sandy) Woodward GBE, KCB, commands: H.M. Submarine 'Tireless' 1960; 'teacher' of Perisher Courses 1967; H.M.Submarine 'Warspite' 1969; Falklands War, Aircraft Carrier Task Group 1982; Flag Officer Submarines and NATO Commander Submarines Eastern Atlantic 1983: Commander-in-Chief Naval Home Command 1987: Flag Aide-de-Camp to H.M. the Queen.

because 'Sea Scouts' coxswain's daughter led the team. Enough said.

Anway, my answer was that I would join if he could convince Tireless's skipper to do so as well. Seeming a little put out that he hadn't been himself in the frame he asked why. "Well sir, I know that if there was a question I couldn't answer, then Lieutenant Commander Woodward would". In the end the whole thing fizzled out, a bit of a damp squib, we didn't send a team as probably we lacked the necessary brain power.

Further up the creek we were even more laid back with our dress code, so much so that one forenoon, both boats being at the jetty, I was invited down to Tireless's forrard mess at 'up spirits' by my counterpart her killick RP2. One of their mess members said he always thought I was Australian Navy. Being a guest and a rum rat to boot, I didn't point out that that was a strange deduction for him to make, as I habitually wore a Canadian Navy issue denim jacket, which had 'Canada' flashes sewn on each shoulder.

I don't know if our skipper climbed to the highest rungs of the slippery pole, but he was regarded by the crew as a very safe pair of hands, or eyes, and that's what mattered most to us, also his was a very pleasant personality, a rare mixture.

Our First Lieutenant, tall reddish hair, known by us as 'Ginger', but not to his face, was quite aloof and a little haughty, but apart from that we all held him in high regard. I know he didn't make admiral as twenty or so years down the line I saw him on telly. He, as a four ringed Captain (retired), was naval spokesman for Jaynes Publications, the bible for all things naval worldwide.

I have beaten around the bush a bit to get to the actual event or accidental misadventure. We were somewhere toward the north of Norway exercising with NATO forces, were dived and snorting, standing charge starboard running charge port. This meant we were propelling on the port diesel, giving us enough speed to keep station on some fishing boats in our vicinity, while generating through our main motors to feed plenty of amps to our hungry batteries.

I was in my 'office' the radar shack, a cupboard-like enclosure, aft of the control room. The seaguard aerial was raised but not rotating or transmitting. That, the snort head and the periscope would give a similar radar profile as would the fishing boats and hopefully fool 'enemy' forces. Every so often I would be ordered to take one all round sweep, to give range of these fishing boats and see whatever else might be in the vicinity. I think at the time we had problems with the shuff-duff, otherwise I would have certainly been monitoring that. My door was shut and I was in a little cocoon, a world of my own.

The boat gradually took on a bow up angle, nothing particularly unusual, but before long the angle became more pronounced and we stopped snorting. The pounding of the two diesel engines, not far aft of where I sat, ceased. The more pronounced angle suddenly became alarmingly acute. Glancing over my right shoulder at my depth gauge, I saw that we were at about 150ft and obviously slipping backwards, downwards. Already the stern would be close to our safe diving depth, which had been limited due to the boat's age.

I slid open my door, that is to say I released the handle and the door did its own sliding, doing exactly what Isaac Newton said it would. Clinging to overhead pipework I pulled myself into the Control Room, the crew at their controls were all clinging on, Jack Rabbit at the steering position had turned a whiter shade of pale – most eyes were on the Jimmy – our Mr Cool. He was sending pumping and flooding signals via the light indicator box to the main ballast pump operator and with the captain's permission ordered HP air to be blown into no. 6 and no. 4 main ballast tanks. The captain had been summoned to the control room at an early stage, but to give him credit, seeing that the Jimmy was taking the right actions, he assumed more of an advisory role. As soon as the ballast tank buoyancy began to take effect the main vents had to be opened to release the air and allow the tanks to flood with seawater again. The object being to regain some control over the submarine's fore and aft trim, not to break surface, especially as we were on a war footing, albeit an exercise.

This fore and aft trim would be achieved by removing water ballast from 'Z' tank back aft and counterbalancing by flooding water into 'A' trim tank up forrard. Reports were coming in from all compartments to confirm we were shut off for going deep, I had already anticipated this, as when leaving the radar office I had shut off my shallow water depth gauge. Other reports were coming in to confirm we had watertight integrity.

Realising that my seaguard aerial was still raised and trying to sound matter of fact, I requested "Permission to lower seaguard, Sir". Jimmy, sounding matter of fact without trying, replied "Yes, please lower seaguard".

The drama was not yet over, before full control was established, more blowing of main ballast and its subsequent venting was carried out, far from ideal as the sound of it would carry for miles, a sonic boon for searching sonars.

Normality returned eventually, the tension eased and we resumed snorting to complete our charge. We had broached the surface slightly, but hadn't compromised our position or sunk any fishing boats. A post mortem would be held as no evidence of water ingestion had been found. The submarine and especially the batteries were not designed for these acute angles. The consequences of battery acid leakage could be lethal.

Later, when back in harbour, the captain cleared lower deck, including chiefs and P.O's. We mustered in the fore-ends. He didn't talk down to us or lecture us, just pointed out that the boat had suffered mishaps in her long career and he wanted to see her safely through her final months. It seems a valve or valves in the trim line had been left open, allowing water to flow aft at an increasing rate as the angle was increased by the flow. We shuffled about a bit in embarrassment, but submariners are a stoic bunch on the whole and we took it on the chin. I think these incidents are more prone to happening when in the training role as we now were.

This submarine, the Talent, had been swept from dry dock at Chatham in December 1954, when the caisson sealing no. 3 dock collapsed. She had 50 persons on board with the hatches open. She was washed across the Medway onto sand banks, rescue was slow as night had fallen. Four men died and thirty men were injured, many quite seriously.

About 18 months later Talent was damaged in collision with a warship, while dived south of the Isle of Wight (8 May 1956).

The Royal Navy has lost 31 submarines to date during peacetime, many with all, or a high proportion of their crew. Three of this total were 'T' class.

If you've got a black cat, He's got a panther

One sunny morning, sitting around the escape hatch on the forecasing, our only forum for inter-mess repartee, social dialogue, call it what you will, it was an outlet for young men cooped up, often with no window to the outside world. We didn't even merit an occasional peep through the periscope, even to sight the surface of the sea that we sailed below. As I wrote before, our equivalent of the office worker's drinks machine – except we had no drinks to drink or even the machine, all we had was a mountain of spuds to peel.

I related to my captive audience an incident that occurred during a taxi ride between Portland and Weymouth some time before. I had gone ashore with my oppo, Tansy Lee. We called in for a quick one at the Breakwater Bar, just outside the base, it would fortify us during the bus ride to Weymouth. At the bar, also on their way to Weymouth, was Polly Parrot, our coxswain, and the T.I. Polly, being Polly and a generous man to boot, bought us both a pint, probably because he knew he had worked us half to death during the day, but also I think it was because he wanted us to go 50-50 for the taxi fare to Weymouth. This is what we decided to do, the beer had worked its magic.

The taxi had just crossed the Chesil Beach when its left rear tyre burst and we skidded to a halt. By this time we were late for whatever Polly and the T.I. were planning to do. The cab driver, who had rummaged through his boot for the jack, suddenly remembered it was at home in his garage. Polly, usually a mild mannered man, blew his fuse. "I hope you've got a bloody wheel brace" stormed Polly, "Right, good then loosen the wheel nuts and get ready with the spare, when I lift the car up stick the wheel on".

Now Polly was built like a bull. He grasped the underside of the body and hoiked the taxi off the ground – mind you he made us passengers get out first. Job done, wheel on and off we went. Polly demanded and got a 50% discount on the fare.

As I finished my narrative, Dodger Long piped up "Bloody T.I, if you've got a black cat, he's got a panther, When I told him I had boxed the army fly-weight champ he said, that's nothing, I've boxed against Randolph Turpin. He used to be a killik chef at St Vincent the same time I was in training there".

Coming to the T.I's defence the tanky said "Turpin was there just before he turned pro and won the middleweight championship of the world. He used to spar with the boys in the gym".

Not to be outdone Jock Brodie said "I knew Russ Conway when he was in the Andrew. We served on an inshore mine-sweeper together, but I never heard him play piano."

It turned out they all knew someone famous except me, I only knew Polly Parrot. He was a good coxswain, well at least he was the only one that ever bought me a pint.

A Wind of Change blowing under The ocean

I was up at Faslane when the nuclear powered USS 'Nautilas' arrived on her maiden voyage which included the first underwater crossing of the north polar ice cap.

Again I happened to be at Faslane when our first nuclear submarine HMS 'Dreadnought' arrived. I went aboard her by invitation of a crew member I knew from my training days. It was the only time I have ever set foot on a nuclear powered submarine. Her reactor had been provided by the US Admiral Rickover, the father of their nuclear programme, spurred by his friendship with Lord Mountbatten.

During the 1960's ten nuclear powered submarines were designed and built for the Royal Navy. Their crews were trained and the boats went on operations in support of N.A.T.O. during the cold war. These could be anti-submarine operations against the Soviet Navy or deterrent patrols carrying inter-continental, nuclear warhead armed, missiles.

From a late start, our designers and ship constructors have caught up with and in many ways have surpassed both the Americans and the Russians, if not in numbers then certainly in the quality of the submarines now in service.

This has been an achievement only equaled by the professionalism of the crews of our now all nuclear service, which has also taken over ballistic missile deterrent from the R.A.F.

We were a stop gap, using World War II boats and having to make do. I could sense the wind of change blowing under the ocean. Quite rightly, I believe, the scarce money and resources were earmarked for the nuclear programme. Equally scarce manpower were on long training courses to man the boats that were under construction.

In 1963 when I was recommended by my then First Lieutenant to go forward for selection as a candidate for training as a special duties officer, I had set myself a target of obtaining eight G.C.E.s. I already had some service equivalents, the H.E.T.s, then I took and passed two G.C.E.s once back in the U.K, which left me two more to take.

It was for this reason that I was now sitting in our Captain's cabin, on his seat at his little writing desk, as this was the only place on the submarine that was both fairly quiet and also private.

The sealed papers had come aboard in the Captain's briefcase and it was typical of the thoughtfulness of the man that he allowed the use of his cabin for the purpose and also it was indicative of the encouragement shown by the officers of the Service, towards anyones desire for advancement.

I don't suppose there are many certificates that show the exam was taken aboard a submarine, one of mine is marked H.M. submarine Talent, Spring 1965, the other H.M. submarine Talent, November 1965. On both occasions we were dived, this time I could see from the depth gauge at the foot of the Captain's bunk, we were at 250ft and proceeding slowly, straight and level, obviously in deference to me. I had done no studying toward any of the G.C.E. exams, I just took the exams, which is probably why I didn't get the highest grades in some subjects.

Sitting here it was quite eerie and a little surreal, it, being a quieter place, I could hear a trickling sound as the boat moved through the water. For a leader at the pinnacle of his profession the Captain had no luxury, a bunk not much different in comfort than ours, a small wardrobe for his uniforms and a wash-hand basin. The Captain had his own steward to serve him his meals and to provide hot drinks, if, as quite often, he spent hour upon hour in the control room during attacks, or on the bridge during fog or at busy choke points. It was his steward I had tried to persuade to serve me a coffee on the little silver salver he used to serve our officers and dignitaries if, on some flag wagging visits to U.K. or foreign ports, we held a cocktail party in the control room. He would have none of it, using the excuse that I wasn't to be disturbed during the exam or have any contact that could be misconstrued as cheating.

To give the steward his due, he didn't forget his lower deck roots, or perhaps it was because he resided in the forrard mess of which I was the killik in charge, as when a cocktail party was in full swing he would place a bottle of brandy someplace where, during our sentry's hourly patrol through the boat, it could be spirited away. He did insist we put the empty bottle back before the party's end, because the Jimmy used them as his accounting tool for the wardroom's wine and spirits usage that he was responsible for. I think with his skills he went on to work for H.M. Treasury on his retirement.

'They' in the control room were drinking what they called 'horses necks' a cocktail of brandy and dry ginger – we did the same but left out the ginger. Now I've found from experience that wine doesn't always travel well, but distil it into cognac and it tastes even better for its journey down from the upper yard to the lower deck. It helped to iron out the bumps of inequality, after all we cleaned the control room before and after the party.

I was looking more toward using these exams as some kind of proof of educational standard for a career outside of the Service, the nine year engagement I had signed up for was fast coming to an end, the three years served before age 18 years did not count. Like many others of my branch I was disgruntled as promotion for leading rates was virtually frozen. Over the previous three years while waiting my promotion to Petty Officer to come through, I had seen countless youngsters of other branches, who I helped to get through their submarine part 3 qualification, get promoted first to leading electrician or leading engineering mechanic and then within months to Petty Officer rate of their particular branch. The next thing I could be reporting to them if they were duty P.O.

My advancement to special duties officer would mean me reverting to general service as submarines only had officers of the general list, not only that I would have to change specialization to either gunnery or anti-submarine warfare because the radar branch did not have special duties officers. If I decided to stay as I was in submarines I would have to take a nuclear course as that was the future of the service, diesel electric submarines would soon be a thing of the past.

The wind of change was going to blow me ashore, so I began to ponder my chances in civilian life. This was all I knew, having gone straight from school to the Navy. But who would need a submarine service, radar plot specialist – not Henry Ford or Thomas Bata, that's for sure. I didn't fancy another uniformed career in the police, fire service, or as a prison officer, having steered clear of regimentation in the Navy.

Being a married man, I now had a wife to consider in my future plans, as we both had ambition to own our own home and not be in married quarters, beholden to the Navy. I was fortunate that she would back me, whatever I decided to do.

On the 22nd October 1966 the medals, clasps and gratuity section of my service documents were anoted C.C.B. No, this was not some decoration I had been awarded for meritorious service. It stood for civilian clothing benefit. I travelled to a tailors shop close to Woking station, to be fitted with civilian clothes.

The next day I joined the rat race, how I fared, as they say, is another story.

2013

A rolling stone drops anchor

I had been something of a rolling stone since leaving the Navy at the age of 27, finding it difficult to settle down as every couple of years I was looking toward new horizons and a new challenge. There were a number of things in my favour which enabled me to lead this lifestyle. Firstly my wife never stood in my way and after we'd gone through the pro's and con's, she would back me 100%. Jobs were plentiful and my H.E.T.'s and G.C.E.'s were a help so I was able to move on if the urge took me. Some of the jobs meant working away from home for long periods.

The coming of our two children obviously changed my outlook somewhat as I didn't want to be an absent father remote from the family scene, also I had determined to be settled if possible in a permanent pensionable career by the age of 35 which in those days would give me 30 years to build a reasonable pension pot.

Cutting out some time and detail, chance and coincidence was again to play a part if my life. I had been given the name of the person responsible for recruiting security and other technical and services staff into Lloyds Bank, although I was also told that it was difficult to get in as standards were high and these few opportunities in great demand. I managed to reach Ron Martin on the 'phone and he asked me my background and experience. I said I was ex-Navy. "So was I" he said. Anyway it turned out that he also served in submarines, my last boat Talent he had served on as his first boat, during its first commission in the far east, towards the end of the war against Japan. I'm not saying our common experience had any bearing on my landing a job with the bank, where I worked for 24 years and from which I have now been long retired.

The city branch of the Royal British Legion within Lloyds Bank must have been one of the Legion's largest branches. It was very active and had high level leadership with support right up to board level within the Bank. Along with most other technical and services staff I was a branch member and there were many members from within clerical and other areas of the Bank.

When I heard of the 'Submarine Memorial Appeal' whose plan was to save and preserve the 'A' class submarine Alliance from a fate suffered by others of her class at the scrap yard, I enlisted the enthusiastic support of the branch to help raise money for the cause. A considerable sum was raised throughout our branch and other branches within the Bank. Lloyds Bank had at that time a 'pound for pound' policy which meant that they doubled the sum we collected. Below is a copy 'thank you' letter from the Appeal director which is something of an historical document in its own right.

I never served on the Alliance but I did serve on the Aurochs the same class but without any streamlining. The only time I had seen Alliance was in Singapore, she was sporting camouflaged paint and had a deck gun fitted for use during the Indonesian campaign. Alliance had conducted investigations into the equatorial current, a subject I had mentioned in my chapter regarding the make up of the oceans themselves. I am pleased to have played a small part in the preserving of HMS Alliance.

'If You Can't Take A Joke…You Shouldn't Have Joined' was printed by Srinivas Fine Arts (P) Ltd, the leading Indian print and book technology company and their 'Nightingale' branded products are the finest in paper. The books were shipped from their factory at Sivakasi, Tamil Nadu to Tuticorin a feeder port on India's southern tip and then on to the container port of Colombo, Sri Lanka. The books formed a tiny part of the cargo of a massive container ship of over 72,000 gross tons and a length of over 290m. The arrival port was Southampton from where they were transported to my storage and handling facility at Brentwood, Essex.

The container ship's route was very much the same as HMS Superb's on her voyage home to Chatham from what was then Ceylon. A lot of water has flowed around Cape Aghulas during those 56 years.